SOUTH AFRICA
Coming of Age under Apartheid

South Africa

Coming of Age under Apartheid

Jason Lauré and Ettagale Lauré
Photographs by Jason Lauré

FARRAR STRAUS GIROUX
NEW YORK

Library of Congress Cataloging in Publication Data
Lauré, Jason.
  South Africa, coming of age under apartheid.
  SUMMARY: *Interviews with eight South African*
young people of various ethnic backgrounds show
the effect of apartheid on their lives.
  1. South Africa—Race relations—Juvenile
literature. 2. Youth—South Africa—Juvenile
literature. [1. South Africa—Race relations]
I. Lauré, Ettagale, joint author. II. Title.
DT763.L33 968'.004 79-23109
ISBN 0-374-37146-6

Contents

• Windhoek

Walvis Bay

NAMIBIA
(SOUTH-WEST AFRICA)

BOTSWANA

ORANGE RIVER

REPUBLIC OF

SOUTH AFRICA

ATLANTIC OCEAN

Cape Province

Saldanha Bay

Graaff Rein

MILES   50   100   150   200   250
0
KILOMETERS   100   200

LITTLE KAROO
Cape Town

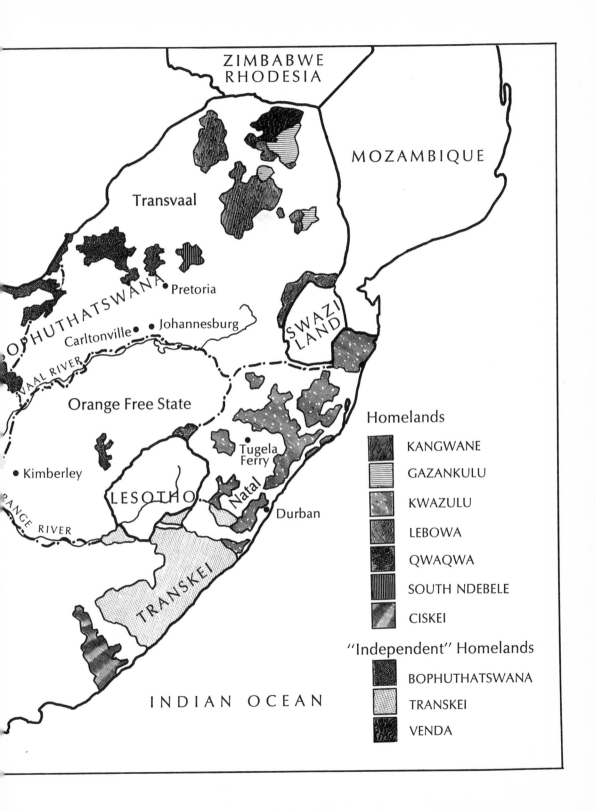

ZIMBABWE
RHODESIA

MOZAMBIQUE

Transvaal

OPHUTHATSWANA
•Pretoria

Carltonville• •Johannesburg

SWAZI
LAND

VAAL RIVER

Orange Free State

•Kimberley

Tugela
Ferry

Natal

LESOTHO

•Durban

ORANGE RIVER

TRANSKEI

INDIAN OCEAN

Homelands

KANGWANE

GAZANKULU

KWAZULU

LEBOWA

QWAQWA

SOUTH NDEBELE

CISKEI

"Independent" Homelands

BOPHUTHATSWANA

TRANSKEI

VENDA

SOUTH AFRICA
Coming of Age under Apartheid

One

After Soweto

In search of South Africans

In 1976, students in South Africa staged a protest, a protest that led to the deaths of more than seven hundred black people. It was a protest against the enforced use of Afrikaans, one of South Africa's two official languages, in schools for blacks, and it began in Soweto, the black township adjoining Johannesburg.

One year later we started out from the United States intending to tell the story of South Africa, knowing it could only be told by living in the country, among the people. So we decided to go to southern Africa for a year, to travel in South Africa, Zimbabwe Rhodesia, South-West Africa/Namibia, Lesotho, and Swaziland, to meet young people from the different racial and ethnic groups living there. We hoped that among them we would find eight individuals to represent the spirit of their various cultures.

As our plane touched down at Jan Smuts Airport in Johannesburg, we were apprehensive. Would we find those young people and would they be willing to talk to us? We had no special introductions, only a desire to become involved in their lives and to tell their stories honestly, stories of coming of age under apartheid.

Apartheid (*a-'par-tate*), the policy of the separate development of races and ethnic groups instituted by South Africa's all-powerful white-minority government, shapes every aspect of life in the country. We didn't have to seek out examples of apartheid. When we set out for Cape Town, we bought our train tickets in the "whites only" section of the terminal. For the 900-mile overnight journey, we traveled in a "whites only" car. Everywhere in South Africa, facilities are labeled for whites and "non-whites," a chilling catchall word that defines the vast majority of the people in the country negatively, not as what they are, but as what they are not. White is the standard against which all others are judged. Even some whites don't come up to the standard of the Afrikaners, a group whose ancestors first came to South Africa in 1652 and who sometimes refer to themselves as the "white tribe" of Africa. Most people reject that term, because the Afrikaners are not descended from a single source but represent a mingling of Dutch, French, German, and other white groups, nor have they ever lived tribally, like the black people of South Africa. But in this way the Afrikaners even reject the other whites of South Africa. Again and again, during our year in South Africa, we confronted the barriers of apartheid.

As the train pulled out of Johannesburg, a modern city about a mile above sea level, ringed by multi-laned highways and dotted with skyscrapers, the landscape changed. From this city, the view soon became one of flat land covered with long grass and tall trees, all on a high plateau that drops slowly from the interior of the country. By midnight we were at a major train interchange, where steam and diesel trains converge from all over South Africa. In the morning we woke in the vast semi-desert of the Karoo, a land covered with scrub bushes. The train crossed the barrier of the Hex

Mountains, revealing the green lowlands that approach Cape Town and the Atlantic Ocean.

From Cape Town we drove out to a temporary camp, constructed by blacks, called Crossroads. A strong, acrid mineral smell rises from the salt flats, once a desolate no-man's-land, undesirable because of the sandy soil and the pervasive smell. In one of the more than two thousand tin houses, we met a teacher in the Crossroads grade school, who sent one of the local youngsters with us out on the dusty paths to find some young women she knew. The first one we spoke to suggested another, and then a third, until finally, there was Nombulelo Princess Fuma (*nom-boo-'lay-lo 'foo-ma*), full of spirit, an adolescent soon to be a mature Xhosa woman. With an interpreter, the tale of Princess's life was unraveled.

Out across the dry inland terrain near the Little Karoo, Daniel Dewet Giliomee (*de-'vet 'heel-o-mee*), an Afrikaner, showed us his family's sheep farm. During our first interview with Dewe (*dee'-vee*) we had a meal with his family, joining them in a simple prayer of thanks for the food. The religious spirit of that moment was in startling contrast to Dewe's blunt discussion of the blacks and Coloureds who worked on the farm.

In Athlone, a Cape Town suburb, we met Debbie Hermanus, a soft-spoken Cape Coloured girl. After talking with Debbie and her family and friends, we took her to visit her grandmother in Salt River. There, in the cheerful kitchen of her little apartment, she brought generations of the history of the Coloured people alive for us.

In Pinetown, a lovely white suburb just a few miles away from Athlone, lives Kathy Boraine, an English-speaking white. Kathy shared with us her feelings of frustration at the way apartheid defined the limits of her attempts to meet with and help the blacks. When Kathy told us she had been out to Crossroads, helping to distribute food and clothing to the blacks, we thought of Princess. The system of apartheid was never clearer than in the contrast between the lives of these two teenagers.

We left the Cape and by private plane, bus, train, and car made our way north, through hundreds of miles of desert, to Oshakati, in SWA/Namibia, a territory governed by South Africa. Our destination was a South African army base, just sixteen miles from the border with Angola. There we found Basil (B.J.) Johnson, a young soldier. With B.J. and other

soldiers from his unit, we drove even closer to the border, to a temporary base from which the men went out on patrol. We made the trip in a special open truck. The V-shaped body of the vehicle was specially adapted to deflect mines. We were securely strapped into our seats by protective restraints.

When we left B.J., we headed southeast, back into the Republic of South Africa, flying to Johannesburg. Then it was off, by car, to KwaZulu, homeland of the Zulu people, in Natal. In the town of Tugela Ferry, where the gold mines maintain a recruiting office, we met Mthokozeni Khyzwayo (*m-'toko-za-nee ka-'zwi-o*), a young Zulu who had just left his kraal, the traditional family compound, to apply for work in the mines. Some weeks later we drove to Carltonville, about an hour from Johannesburg, to the mine, to catch up with him on the job. At both locations, recruiting officials fluent in Zulu translated his words. Though Mthoko and Princess spoke some English, they preferred to speak their own languages during our lengthy interviews.

From KwaZulu we drove to Durban, on the Indian Ocean, where most of South Africa's Indians live. At the University of Durban–Westville, we met a group of theater students and one of them told us about his younger cousin, Symanthia. That very day we met Symanthia in the Indian section of Durban, where she lived with her parents and two sisters. Soon we were learning about her world of university studies, religion, and dancing.

Leaving the subtropical climate and beach-front hotels of Durban, we made our way inland once again, this time to Ulundi, the capital of KwaZulu. At a three-day meeting of Inkatha, the black cultural movement, we were given an introduction to Lukhetho Buthelezi (*loo-'kay-to boo-ta-'lay-zee*), who lives in Soweto.

We asked Lukhetho to talk with us in our Johannesburg hotel, one of a handful where the different races are allowed to meet. He came after he finished work, and we began our interview. Late on that first night, we took Lukhetho home to Soweto. Out of Johannesburg we drove, past warehouses on the edge of the city, into increasingly desolate areas. Then, at the edge of the road, we were confronted by a big green sign, warning us, in both English and Afrikaans, that no one can enter Soweto without a permit. It was the only sign that indicated Soweto existed. Not one directional sign shows you how to get there.

We were acutely aware of our white skins as Lukhetho directed us to drive straight ahead, into the vast black township of one and a half million inhabitants. We could see the dark forms of a burned-out post office and other buildings destroyed or damaged during the protests. We didn't see any of the houses at first, because most of the homes in Soweto do not have electricity. The lights from the state-run bars, from the few streetlamps and our car provided the only illumination. On our return, as we drove back through the night to Johannesburg, we thought of Lukhetho's tears of frustration as he related some of the incidents of his life. We returned to Soweto several times, once meeting Lukhetho's girlfriend Manono.

And finally, we traveled to Swaziland, a small, black-ruled country nearly surrounded by South Africa, to talk with students who fled Soweto during the 1976 uprising. The young women we met were too fearful to talk with us, and even as we were explaining our work to them, the matron of their school slipped out and notified the local authorities. We were detained briefly by the police, to discourage any further contact with the student-refugees. Apartheid seemed to have followed us to Swaziland, keeping us separate from these black South Africans.

These stories are part of history now, for history is just what happened yesterday. Each of our eight youngsters is isolated in his or her life, divided by apartheid, as the country itself is divided. The way in which "our kids" live is determined by the laws of apartheid and by the traditions of their cultures. To help you understand these profiles, to explain how the roots of apartheid lie deep in the country's past, we must present some of the historical background of South Africa.

Two

South Africa

The laager

THE REPUBLIC of South Africa is the southernmost region of the African continent. It sprawls from the Indian Ocean on the east to the Atlantic Ocean on the west and embraces a variety of climates, ranging from subtropical to desert. Within its boundaries, in a land mass about one-eighth the size of the United States, live some 26 million people. Four provinces make up South Africa: the Cape Province, the Orange Free State, the Transvaal and Natal, plus the enclave of Walvis Bay, all bound together under a parliamentary system of national government. Rich in mineral resources, South Africa lacks only oil to be self-sufficient. Although a large part of the country is desert or semi-arid, much of the nation enjoys a moderate climate. It has excellent harbors and enough arable land to provide for all its food needs. Such a well-favored nation could be the leader of the African continent and a positive influence in the world community. But South Africa is neither.

Almost universally, South Africa is condemned for its racial policy of apartheid, a policy aimed at separating the races and ethnic groups that inhabit the country: white, black, Indian, and "Coloured" (mixed). Four and a half million whites have the right to vote; they rule themselves and also the remaining twenty-one and a half million "non-whites," who are denied the vote.

Documented histories begin from the time the whites arrived in South Africa, because the people who were native to the land, the Khoikhoi and the San, did not have written language. Little of their oral history found its way into the written European record.

Though ships had been stopping at the Cape of Good Hope for some two hundred years, the first permanent base was established by the Dutchman Jan van Riebeeck, who arrived at the Cape on April 6, 1652. He was sent to establish a reliable supply of fresh vegetables, meat, and water for the ships of the Dutch East India Company, en route to India and the East.

These first Dutch settlers exploited the Khoikhoi and abused the San, but were unable to make them into laborers and servants. So, in 1657, they began to bring in slaves from Java and Sumatra and, later, blacks from East Africa and Madagascar. The mingling of all those groups, including the whites, produced a new racial mixture, the Coloureds.

The second group of Europeans to arrive at the Cape, one hundred and fifty French Huguenots, was sent by the Dutch East India company in 1689. There were then about seventeen hundred whites at the Cape.

The physical isolation of the Cape was an important element in shaping its new inhabitants. Not exposed to the continual flow of ideas and experimentation going on among the peoples of Europe, the Cape dwellers did not advance much beyond the thinking of the seventeenth century. The white farmers, or Boers, were already moving away from the Cape peninsula, in search of more farmland, and to get away from the restrictive Dutch East India Company. These inland family groups became even more rigid in their thinking as they lost contact with other settlers and their language began to change, becoming the forerunner of Afrikaans, the language spoken by 60 percent of the whites in South Africa today.

As they made their way toward the interior, the Boers came into contact with black groups already established there. Artifacts found in the Transvaal indicate that blacks lived in the area as long ago as the year 1000. Various other ethnic groups were moving down from central Africa, to escape the slavers supplying American, European, and African markets.

Others were constantly on the move, seeking new grazing for their cattle. By the mid-1700s, clashes between Boers and blacks were frequent. A series of wars, starting around the third quarter of the century, lasted a hundred years, during which the blacks were almost always defeated.

Though the Dutch held the Cape without challenge for about a hundred and fifty years, its strategic position in the world's sea lanes was not lost on Britain, a formidable sea power. Using the excuse of a commitment to the Dutch, who were then fighting the French in Europe, the British invaded the Cape colony in 1795. Initially welcomed, they were later resisted by the Dutch. By 1806, the British were permanently in charge at the Cape, which became a British colony.

From the start, Boer and British clashed in temperament, life style, and culture. The Boers lived in the early 1800s much as their ancestors had at the end of the 1600s, though they had already migrated as far inland as Graaff Reinet, 400 miles east of Cape Town.

The Boers chafed under the growing British influence and rule, which threatened not only their way of life but also their belief in the superiority of white over black. The British, for example, also practiced slavery, but they encouraged slaves to bring complaints of ill treatment to court. The breaking point came in 1834, when the British outlawed slavery in South Africa, as they had outlawed it at home and in their other colonies. The Boers, who lived according to a strict, literal interpretation of the Bible, saw this move as a direct attack on their view of themselves as a chosen people, a race predestined to rule.

Several thousand Boers broke away from the Cape. They loaded all their possessions onto ox-drawn wagons and, with their families, set out for the interior. This exodus became known as the Great Trek. The Boers trekked to preserve their way of life. Spurred on by the women, who were the force behind educating the children to read the Bible, they hauled their wagons over formidable mountain barriers, often having to take the wheels off the wagons, unhitch the oxen, and then physically pull the wagons over particularly bad spots. The trek itself strengthened their convictions and led to a fanatical belief in the righteousness of their actions. But in their push north and east, away from the British, the Boers were heading for a different kind of battle, a battle against blacks for the right to the land.

Their first encounters were with the Xhosa, but the great test would be with the Zulus, who had become a terrifying fighting force under the leadership of the legendary Shaka. Today their descendants evoke the pride of those warring days.

On December 16, 1838, Boers and Zulus met in an encounter that is a landmark in South Africa's history. Each group assumed its classic fighting stance. The Zulu soldiers advanced in a precise pattern, chanting as they attacked, to sustain the tension. The Boers fell back to their traditional defense position, drawing their sixty-four wagons into a laager. Wagon wheels were locked together, forming an impenetrable circle, and thornbushes were placed between, to complete the barricade. Men took their firing positions; women stayed behind to reload the weapons. Children and animals were kept well inside the safety of the laager. Armed with superior weapons, and from the protection of the laager, the Boers killed three thousand Zulus. A nearby river ran red with blood, giving a name to the encounter: the Battle of Blood River. Only three Boers, it is claimed, were killed in the assault.

Before the battle, the Boers had prayed, making a covenant with God that if they lived they would forever after honor that day. The Day of the Covenant has become a cornerstone of Boer folklore, celebrated annually at the Voortrekker Monument erected near Pretoria a hundred years after

the battle. For the Zulus, it is Dingaan's Day, a time of mourning for the Zulu dead who fought for their leader Dingaan, the successor to Shaka.

An estimated fourteen thousand Boers, a fifth of the white population of the Cape, emigrated during the ten-year period starting in 1835. As they moved inland, crossing first the Orange River and then the Vaal, the Boers established the Orange Free State and the Transvaal. Those Boers who trekked as far east as the coast were subdued by the British, who also overwhelmed the black groups who lived along the fertile Indian Ocean shore. This territory, known as Natal, was annexed by the British in 1843. They established sugarcane plantations, hoping to use the labor of blacks living in the territory. But the blacks were traders whose cattle could be exchanged for other goods. They had no need to take paid work. The sugarcane growers persuaded the government to bring in contract laborers from India, and the first group, numbering six thousand, arrived in 1860. Thousands more followed, and by the end of the century there were thirty thousand Indians in South Africa.

The Afrikaners' desire for isolation was thwarted not only by the presence of the blacks but also by the discovery of diamonds in 1867 and gold in 1886. Eager to take advantage of this wealth, the British tried to gain political control of the Transvaal.

The conflict over the newfound wealth finally drove the Boers and the British to war. After a hundred years of increasing bitterness and hostility, the two groups met in battle. The first Anglo-Boer War, 1880–81, was of minor importance, but the outcome of the Anglo-Boer War of 1899–1902 determined the political structure of South Africa in the twentieth century.

At the start, the Boer army numbered about 30,000 and the British no more than 25,000. But by 1900 the British had brought 150,000 men into the battle zone, and ultimately involved the staggering total of 450,000 men against 90,000 Boers. It was a guerrilla action in which British numbers finally overcame the Boers' superior knowledge of the land. The losses were not only on the field of battle. In one of the most shameful incidents in British and South African history, tens of thousands of Boer women and children were interned in British camps. With hardly any provision for food, shelter, sanitation, and medical care, an estimated 25,000 died from starvation and disease.

Finally, on May 31, 1902, the Boers surrendered to the British, who, in victory, were magnanimous. The two white groups needed to present a united front to the ever-growing numbers of blacks. Although English had been the only official language since 1828, the British gave Afrikaans official recognition, and eventually granted it equal status. (The eight black languages were never granted recognition at all.) Through this gesture, and through other moves toward reconciliation, the British and the Afrikaners joined together on May 31, 1910, to form the Union of South Africa. In just eight years the two former enemies overcame their enmity to unite against what they perceived as a greater problem: to keep the "natives" in their place. In the next years, that "place" would be clearly and severely defined.

An all-white Parliament was established, which began a systematic, legal denial of rights to the blacks. Black attempts to form their own groups, such as the African National Congress, were legislated against by the Afrikaners' National Party, formed in 1913. From the start, the Afrikaners acted to prevent any attempt by the blacks to form themselves into a powerful unit. White South Africans are said to fear *swartgevaar*—"the black peril." They see the blacks washing over them in a great black tide, because blacks greatly outnumber them. Early in this century, there were three blacks to one white. Today the ratio is four to one, and it continues to grow. At each election, party leaders raised the specter of *swartgevaar*, and more and more whites voted to endorse the policies of separation which keep the blacks in an inferior positon.

To define the blacks' "place," the white Parliament divided up the land. They took 86.3 percent for the whites; the rest, a mere 13.7 percent, they set aside for the blacks. This 1936 Native Land and Trust Act ignored both Coloureds and Indians. The 13.7 percent was to be further divided into native reserves, for the various black ethnic groups. Later called *bantustans*, these areas are today known as homelands, implying that the blacks belong in those territories. Thus the scene was set to implement the policy of apartheid—separateness.

The word "apartheid" was used for the first time in a newspaper story in 1943. It expressed the idea of total separation of the races, an idea so contrary to the reality of the situation—blacks being the main labor force throughout industry, mining, and agriculture—that one can only stand in dumbstruck disbelief at the determination with which the policy has been pursued.

The bantustans, or homelands in which the blacks are supposed to live, are disconnected bits and pieces of land, "islands" separated by the "ocean" of white South Africa. One such homeland, Bophuthatswana, is scattered over three of South Africa's four provinces. When the whites created the homelands for the blacks, they kept for themselves the most desirable parts, such as the cities, the gold and diamond mining lands, and the ports: in short, the real wealth of the country.

In 1948, the National Party gained a majority of seats in Parliament and the racial policy of South Africa today was given its final, fatal touches. Major pieces of legislation designed to keep the races apart were devised, and relentlessly amended to close any loopholes. In 1949, the government passed the Prohibition of Mixed Marriages Act, making marriage between whites and non-whites illegal. In order to implement this legislation, the government set itself the task of identifying each person by race under the Population Registration Act of 1950. But racial lines had blurred during the three hundred years whites have been at the Cape. The genetic mixing that took place is said to have left traces of color in nearly every South African born there. Yet, in a country where privilege is based on one's color, the difference between being classified black or Coloured is profound. And, in fact, some families were split by the officials who did the classifying—dark Coloureds were classified as black, some light Coloureds were labeled white, and some whites were classified as Coloured. Because the Group Areas Act of 1950 had made it illegal for people of different races to live in the same area, people who were classified as being of a different race from their families were forced to live separately.

Through homelands legislation, whites intended to eliminate blacks from South Africa, but by designating separate group areas for Indians and Coloureds under the Group Areas Act, they conceded the right of these two groups to live within South Africa. The Act also permitted the government to declare an area "white" though Coloureds or Indians lived and owned businesses there. People were forced out of their homes and sent to live in areas designated for them by the white government. This Act and its subsequent amendments forced the removal of a hundred thousand families, primarily Coloureds and Indians, in order to accommodate whites. As they moved out, some of their homes were destroyed and others were renovated for whites. Historic Coloured and Indian sections in Cape Town and Durban were reduced to rubble. At the same time, in an effort to consolidate the homelands into fewer but larger pieces, the government moved nearly two million blacks from their traditional lands, often to barren lands far away. More than two million blacks, Coloureds, and Indians are still to be moved in this staggering effort to separate people.

On February 3, 1960, British Prime Minister Harold Macmillan sent shock waves through the South African Parliament when, in a speech in Cape Town, he predicted: "The wind of change is blowing through this continent." It was an accurate assessment of the rise of black national feelings, feelings that led to demands for independence by the African colonies of France, Portugal, Great Britain, Belgium, and Spain.

The month after Macmillan's speech, Robert Sobukwe, chairman of the newly formed Pan-Africanist Congress, tried to lead a peaceful campaign against the compulsory carrying of reference books, or passes, as they are called. Every black over the age of sixteen must carry a pass which gives in detail his work record and proves his "right" to be in a white city and to live in a black township. It is the single most hated symbol of apartheid. On March 21, 1960, thousands of blacks in the township of Sharpeville marched to the police station to turn in their passes. In a panic, the police opened fire on the vast, unarmed crowd, killing sixty-nine people. The event became known as the Sharpeville massacre.

Sobukwe spent three years in prison on Robben Island for his role in the pass-law demonstrations, and then was held for six more years without a trial. Upon release from prison, Sobukwe was restricted to the Kimberley district. Finally, years of imprisonment, poor food, and inadequate medical care took their toll. Sobukwe died, in Kimberley, at the age of fifty-three. On March 11, 1978, he was buried in the little town of Graaff Reinet, where he was born. His funeral was attended by thousands. For four hours the mourners listened under the clear South African sky, the sun beating down, as speakers representing many factions praised Sobukwe. Then the family walked to the cemetery with the casket, and Robert Sobukwe was

buried in a dusty little scrap of land in the township. Young blacks lined the route to the cemetery, softly chanting a song with a chorus of "Azania, Azania," the ancient territorial name and the name blacks use for a free South Africa.

Following the demonstrations at Sharpeville, both the Pan-Africanist Congress and the African National Congress were banned. In South Africa, "banning" is a form of punishment which can be applied to a person, an organization, or a piece of writing. A banned person lives under a form of house arrest and is restricted to seeing only one person at a time. He may even be restricted to a district that is not his own home. A banned

person may not be quoted, even after his death. A writer may himself be banned, or any or all of his works may be banned. For many, banning means an end to their livelihood and to any normal life.

A year after Sharpeville, on May 10, 1961, white South Africa proclaimed itself a Republic, cutting the last formal ties with the British Commonwealth—thus declaring to the world that it intended to pursue its own policies. Elsewhere in Africa, British Prime Minister Macmillan's "wind of change" prediction was coming true. By 1976, virtually every colony had attained independence, leading to black-majority rule. But in South Africa the white Nationalists continue to consolidate their power.

Until recently, South Africa's white-minority regime was strengthened by the stability of similar political regimes in the countries bordering her. But that stability was shattered when the Portuguese colonies of Mozambique and Angola were granted independence following the 1974 revolution in Portugal. Thousands of Portuguese whites fled the colonies, many going to South Africa, where the Portuguese-speaking population now numbers more than six hundred thousand. In Mozambique one black-majority group immediately took over, but in Angola three factions battled for control in a civil war. Once control was established, a group of black nationalists from South-West Africa/Namibia was able to set up a base in southern Angola. This group, the South-West Africa People's Organization (SWAPO), expanded its fight to free SWA/Namibia and to wrest control of the territory from South Africa.

South Africa has governed SWA/Namibia since 1919, under a mandate of the League of Nations which gave South Africa responsibility for governing these people in their own best interest. Prior to World War I, the territory had been a German protectorate. South Africa imposed a similar system of its own apartheid policy on the territory's nearly one million people, 90 percent of whom are black. When the League was disbanded in 1946, the continued validity of the mandate was questioned. For more than thirty years, South Africa has resisted a United Nations effort to grant SWA/Namibia self-rule. In 1973, the United Nations recognized SWAPO as the only legitimate representative of the people of SWA/Namibia.

As SWAPO escalated the fight for freedom on the border of Angola and SWA/Namibia, South Africa was forced to increase compulsory military service from one year to two for all white males. Instead of serving one five-month stint at the border, many now do two. The "boys on the border" are a symbol of white South Africa's belief that if SWAPO gains control the next war will be on the South African border against SWA/Namibia.

Another kind of war was also being waged within South Africa—the continuation of the struggle fought by Sobukwe, and other blacks, each in his own way. This battle erupted on the streets of Soweto on June 16, 1976, when black students organized a school boycott. The initial grievance was the forced use of Afrikaans as a language of instruction, but the protests continued long after the government gave in on that issue. On the first day of the boycott, police moved into Soweto to put down the protest. A crowd of ten thousand young people had gathered to stage a protest march. Panicked by the sheer size of the crowd, the police began to fire. That day, and in the months of protest that followed, an estimated seven hundred blacks were killed. Thousands of black students fled South Africa during the violence to avoid persecution by the police.

Yet, for most white South Africans, including those who live in Johannesburg, just ten miles away, the protests and the police action were just something to read about in the newspaper. Like people in foreign countries, they did not personally experience the frustration and violence. Their lives, their safety, their property were untouched.

After Soweto, reaction to protests, even peaceful protests, was swift. Bannings and detentions increased. In South Africa, anyone can be detained (put in prison) for an indefinite period of time without any charge being made against him. The person virtually disappears. Following the protests, a chilling pattern began to emerge; one after the other, blacks in detention died under mysterious circumstances.

This new series of deaths in detention can be said to have begun on September 12, 1977, when Steve Biko, founder of the South African Students' Organization (SASO) and the foremost black-consciousness leader of his time, died in detention. Though little known outside South Africa during his life, Biko, in death, became headline news around the world. An official inquiry into the circumstances of Biko's death concluded that no one could be held responsible. But as protests mounted within South Africa, the real circumstances became increasingly difficult to cover up. The government then resorted to its surest weapon: it moved to silence all criticism.

On October 19, 1977, virtually all black organizations were banned.

Their leaders, too, were banned or detained. The bannings and detentions drove opposition even further underground, particularly among the blacks. But opposition to the Afrikaner-dominated white government did not disappear. Within the parliamentary system of government, officially sanctioned opposition exists. Under such vigorous leaders as Helen Suzman and Dr. Alex Boraine, the opposition views of the liberal whites of South Africa are expressed. But the Afrikaners believe that Members of Parliament who oppose the government are traitors, in spite of the fact that they themselves for many years defied the British to gain the position they hold today.

To demonstrate the strength of the Afrikaners in South Africa to the world, and to reaffirm their commitment to apartheid, Prime Minister John Vorster called for early elections. During the campaign, the National Party took advantage of the government's control of all radio stations and the one television channel in the country. Opposing candidates received scant coverage in the government-operated media. Vorster got his vote of confidence. The Nationalists were returned to power by an even larger majority.

Life in South Africa today ranges from the marvelous to the miserable, depending almost entirely on the color of one's skin. It is a society in which money does not guarantee privilege and education does not guarantee position. Whites in South Africa enjoy a freedom that money cannot buy. The denial of these freedoms to blacks is so total it affects every aspect of life.

Some think the easing of petty apartheid—the separation of facilities for whites and people of color—is a beginning toward the ultimate breakdown of apartheid—the separation of the races into townships, group areas, homelands. They are wrong. When change does occur, there is usually one of two reasons behind it. Either there is a desire to present a better image to the outside world, or it has become uneconomic to maintain separate facilities. The basic policy of separateness is stronger today than ever before. A move to allow blacks to attend theaters with whites may be widely heralded as a positive development, but it does not signify a change in the underlying policy. Apartheid continues to be asserted, through persistent emphasis on bringing the black homelands to "independence."

Not all homeland leaders are opposed to independence. Chief Lucas Mangope, Prime Minister of Bophuthatswana, accepted independence for his "country" because he thought he could achieve more for his people. He proudly watched the South African flag come down on independence day, December 6, 1977, and watched the new flag go up. He, and the thousands of Tswanas who came to the celebrations, filled the stadium to take part in the festivities, to see the dances and demonstrations of gymnastics. But all the pomp and ceremony could not disguise the fact that the homeland has not been recognized by any nation other than South Africa, which created it, or that it is not a viable economic or geographic unit. It cannot support the multitude of blacks considered by South Africa to be "citizens" of the homeland. These people live in South Africa, but according to the Parliament that creates the legislation, they are now "foreigners." Included in this category are the millions of blacks who live, and who have lived, in the townships all their lives. Many have never been to a homeland or lived in a rural area. Many have intermarried and can no longer be called Tswana

or Zulu or Xhosa. In fact, less than half of South Africa's blacks live in the rural homelands.

For the leader of the more than five million Zulus, the largest black group in South Africa, "independence" is not acceptable. KwaZulu's Chief Minister Gatsha Buthelezi has refused South Africa's version of independence for the Zulu homeland, a collection of more than thirty separate pieces of land. He sees no reason why the Zulus and all the other blacks in South Africa should not share in the wealth that their labor helps to build. Buthelezi's thoughtful and intelligent leadership has brought him recognition not only among blacks but also among whites, Coloureds, and Indians, and he is seen frequently at important political and social gatherings of the different race groups. He is a vigorous leader in the drive to improve conditions for blacks, Coloureds, and Indians, for all the disadvantaged race groups of South Africa.

So the complications of color are not as clear-cut as black and white. Black and black disagree just as white and white do. Many South African whites, nearly all of them English-speakers, have emigrated out of the country. Once again they find themselves in opposition to the Afrikaners, who, because they are indigenous to South Africa, look to no other country as home. As the professional whites leave, they create a "brain drain." To a very small extent, that gap is being filled by educated blacks who are trickling into jobs once reserved, by law, for whites. But their lives are still ruled by apartheid.

For the majority of South Africans, the *only* issue is apartheid. Apartheid defines the limits of life for blacks, Coloureds, and Indians. With it, the Afrikaners are trying to create a laager once again. And indeed South Africa has become a kind of laager—wagons drawn into a circle, weapons at the ready. This time, though, everyone is inside—blacks, whites, Indians, Coloureds. And they are not at all separate.

Three

Lukhetho Buthelezi

Soweto black

THE BLAZING LIGHTS of the city of Johannesburg can be seen from "Soweto Highway," the two-lane road that starts just under the big M1 highway and runs through a desolate, dark landscape into the black township of Soweto to the southwest. More than a million and a half people live in the township. Less than 25 percent of the homes in Soweto have electricity, yet the lights glow on in the deserted offices of Johannesburg. Row upon row of small brick houses with corrugated tin roofs—matchboxes, they call them—stretch across the 34 grim acres of Soweto. Divided by the West Rand Administrative Board (WRAB) into tribal sections, Soweto's townships bear such names as Orlando, Diepkloof, and Dube. The divisions enable WRAB, the white bureaucracy which administers Soweto, to provide "mother tongue" instruction in the schools, in an effort to bolster tribalism.

Lukhetho Buthelezi lives in Diepkloof, a Zulu area, but he is only half Zulu; his mother is a Xhosa. His pass book identifies him as Zulu. His brother Norbert, two years older, is married to a Swazi. And Lukhetho's girlfriend, Manono, whom he plans to marry in three years, is a Sotho. This

intergroup mixing goes on all over Soweto, confounding the authorities, who claim the ethnic groups must be kept apart or they will be at war with one another.

It is a strange place, Soweto, a city that may not be called a city, a city without supermarkets or department stores. Its name, an acronym derived from South West Townships, merely indicates location, a housing development. For most of the inhabitants of Johannesburg, the white city, it might well be on another planet. Soweto has been developed in such a way that a white person can live in Johannesburg all his life and simply not know where Soweto is. There are no signs leading to it, as there are signs to the plush northern suburbs and to the industrial cities that ring the country's oldest working gold mines. Though there are no signs pointing the way, when you reach Soweto there is a sign warning against unauthorized entry.

Whites may not enter Soweto without a permit. Should a white become friendly with a black—at work, for example—he would break the law if he drove the black home one evening after work, unless he had a permit. Blacks must be out of Johannesburg by eleven o'clock at night. After that time, they can be arrested for violating the pass laws that control the influx of blacks into white areas. No black has the right to be in the white city after that time, unless his employment requires it, as in the case of the blacks who guard the empty buildings at night. All this, and much more, is done so that the blacks and the whites can develop separately, to fulfill the policy of apartheid. Most whites are inconvenienced very little because of this policy. Their servants come to them; all the labor required by the city and its inhabitants files in each morning, as expected. But the policy of apartheid forces blacks, particularly urban blacks like Lukhetho Buthelezi, into a life of endless frustration.

The frustrations have always been there, building, simmering. In 1976, they erupted. The initial issue was the enforced use of Afrikaans as a medium of instruction at the high school level. Half the schoolwork was to be taught in Afrikaans—the language of the Afrikaner, the language of the ruling white National Party, the language that symbolizes oppression to blacks. School strikes started in May, a month before the end-of-term holiday. Early in June, students set fire to a police car when the police tried to detain a student. Protests developed. Students gathered. But through informers in Soweto the police were aware of their intentions. When an estimated ten thousand students massed on June 16 for a protest march, the police opened fire on the crowd. It was the first volley in a series of skirmishes that lasted for months. Schools and government buildings were gutted by firebombs, and students boycotted classes, but they were no match for the police. Unarmed students were gunned down if they looked suspicious, or if they were in large groups. In all, more than seven hundred students died in Soweto. As in the pass-law protests in Sharpeville in 1960, the vast numbers of blacks involved seemed to terrify the police, even though the students had no weapons.

The unrest spread to other black townships around the country through July and August. There were deaths in those townships, too, and close to two hundred schools were damaged or destroyed. Long after the authorities gave in on the issue of Afrikaans, the protests continued, pitting stone-throwing students against police armed with an arsenal of weapons. They came in armored vehicles, in vans, with machine guns and rifles.

In KwaZulu, the Zulu homeland, where Lukhetho was a student in his last year of high school, reports were heard of the deaths in Soweto. "The principal didn't want us to go home for the break at the end of the semester. He threatened us with expulsion. He was afraid we would come back to school in the same defiant mood as those students in Soweto. I said, 'I have to go home. My people may be dying.' I came home on June 26. And I was expelled."

Lukhetho found Soweto in a state of near-war. "There were bullet holes in the cement wall around our home. Thank God, my family was all right. There were hundreds killed, more than seven hundred. I know, I saw the mortuaries in Soweto. There were stacks of bodies, just lying on top of each other. I saw bodies in the street. I saw a person being assaulted. I saw girls being taken away by the police. They pointed a gun at one girl and said, 'Come here.' She tried to run away, and they shot at her, next to her feet. She was so frightened she went to them and they took her into the car. A lot of girls were complaining, but there was nobody to complain to. And they were raped. Nine months later those girls were having Coloured [mixed race] babies. They were sixteen, seventeen, eighteen—where else would they have been with white men?

"We lived hearing gunshots outside our home. I think it wasn't just the students. Someone was trying to keep up the old tribal factions. Some people took it as a game . . . They used to shout at night, 'There are Zulus over here.' My parents were afraid to let any of us go out. Eight of us were living at home then. It was dangerous even during the day. The streets were deserted, it was so quiet. There were so many police."

The uprising was said to have been spontaneously organized and led by the students of Soweto. But Lukhetho thinks otherwise. "It was as if a bigger power was behind all this, pushing these students to do it. They were just schoolchildren, but they were moving around in cars. I think they were being used by the owners of these cars. Someone might have tried to use the students for his own ends. Someone who knew exactly what kind of activities would affect the weak points in the government. It might have been anybody who had the idea, 'Say that these students, so many students, can be rowdy, can riot and burn down all these things, the bars and such, they would cripple the country's economy.' "

On August 11, the students massed for a march into town to the main police station at John Vorster Square. Twenty thousand students gathered. "We started this march from Soweto. And we went as far as New Canada, just on the edge of Soweto. It's a big open space. It was so early—just six o'clock in the morning, but the police were already there when we arrived. In South Africa, they always know in advance that you are going to do something. I saw a guy talking, and all of a sudden they threw tear-gas canisters at him and there was a lot of confusion. I got gassed. It chokes— it's damned unpleasant—your eyes . . . And now all the students who had come from different parts of Soweto were swimming in tear-gas fumes. And this big open space was like a battlefield. I didn't see if they arrested anyone. There were too many people. I was just a drop in the ocean."

When they could, the students threw the tear-gas canisters back at the police. The police started shooting into the crowd. "These protests were supposed to be spontaneous, but the Students' Representative Council would give us orders. I don't know who they represented, we never voted on anything. On such a day we were to go to a place and burn it. Just like that. They had commanded us to march to town. I believe in questioning. They didn't want us to question what they were saying. And they threatened me. So I thought about my family. If I didn't go, they were probably going to burn my house, or they would do something to my family. I had no choice. These people, they were SASO [South African Students' Organization]. The leader of the protest, Tsietsi Mashinini, was a member of SASO. He started all this and inspired the others to follow him." SASO was founded in 1968 by black-consciousness leader Steve Biko, who died in police custody one year after the violence in Soweto.

As the uprising continued through 1976, the scope of the students' fury widened. The more action the police took, the more destruction there was.

The free world reacted with disbelief at the events occurring in Soweto. And the prediction that the students could cripple the economy came true

in a very different way. The violence caused such a crisis of confidence in the ability of the South African government to deal with its own people that investments in South Africa plummeted. American companies alone withheld an estimated $1 billion that would have flowed into South Africa in the year following the riots, if things had been normal.

In Soweto, every one of the fifty offices of the West Rand Administration Board were destroyed. Most of the post offices were burned down. And the bars were burned down. "I don't know why the post offices were burned, but the bars I understand. There are so many bars in Soweto, run by WRAB. A lot of people go and drink there, and when they drink, it's not easy to stop, so a lot of money goes to liquor instead of going to something worthwhile for the family. I don't blame them, in fact. They're poor. They want to drown their worries. So that is why there are so many people drinking, they are drunkards. The students were trying to cut down the amount of drinking and at the same time cripple the bars because that's how WRAB makes its money." The bars are owned and operated by the organization that governs Soweto—WRAB—which brews the beer that is sold. It's a native beer, called Imbamba (Zulu for true beer), and was formerly brewed at home. It is now illegal, however, to brew the beer at home. Before the uprising, WRAB made $6,900,000 a year from beer sales. The year after the disturbances, that figure was halved. The bars were among the first buildings to be rebuilt. One medical clinic operates out of the charred remains of a post office. Of the eleven post offices in Soweto, three remain in operation. "We used to pick up our mail at the post office near our house, not even a five-minute walk away. But now we have to take the bus to Orlando to get our mail."

All through 1976 and into 1977, schooling was disrupted. Lukhetho was due to write his final exams, but the student leaders urged the others not to write, as a continued protest. To Lukhetho, this made no sense. "Bantu education is inferior, yes, but it's all we have. How can we ever have a chance if we remain uneducated? I say let's use this Bantu education to get our freedom." The curriculum for black schools is set by the whites. "Bantu education" is designed to teach blacks what they need to know to serve whites. "Bantu" means "people" in several black languages and is a word the blacks detest.

In 1977, Lukhetho, ignoring the leaders' urgings, wrote his exams. He passed, earning his matriculation, which is equivalent to an American high school diploma. And he started to look for a job. "I was desperate for a job, because I had to help support my brothers and sisters. There are six younger than me and they have to be put through school. My parents cannot do it all themselves. I was looking for any kind of a job. The situation was very bad. I was going into furniture shops, anywhere. I might have ended up as a chauffeur. I used to listen to my brother Norbert talk about his job at IBM, where he works repairing computers. And one day I went in there and filled out the application form."

Lukhetho did not think he would be hired at IBM. Of all the applicants, he was the only one with just a matriculation certificate. All the others were university students or graduates. But Lukhetho scored so high on the test that the management could not believe the results. "They said they wanted me to come in for an interview, but when I got there, they retested me. It was exactly the same test, so I did even better the second time."

Still, IBM was cautious. They hired Lukhetho on a temporary basis, just for a month. "I felt very bad about that." But it was a start and it gave him that all-important stamp in his pass book. "I had to go to 80 Albert Street [the headquarters of WRAB] to get my book stamped. But it was easy, because IBM gave me a letter saying that I was a student trainee, and I had it all completed that same morning." More than any other document, the pass book is the symbol of apartheid in South Africa. Every black must carry one, and he is required to show it on demand to any policeman. It details his work record and establishes his right to be in the city.

When Lukhetho entered IBM, he set foot in the white world. He was not used to dealing with whites as equals, just as most whites are incapable of regarding blacks as equals. The country's apartheid relegates blacks to the subservient position of being laborers for whites, who usually see blacks as houseboys, garden boys, messenger boys, delivery boys—always as "boys."

Active programs to employ blacks in positions usually held by whites are a recent phenomenon. Companies such as IBM offer an unusual opportunity for the two racial groups to interact on some sort of equal footing. But for any black, like Luketho, who enters this world, it's a dual life, a Jekyll and Hyde existence. By day he works in the clean, organized world of IBM, in

a modern office building, filled with electronic equipment. He deals with computer problems and uses computer language to solve them. The IBM building, a soaring brick-and-glass construction, looks across to Carlton Centre, the most elaborate complex of its type in South Africa. An international hotel faces a fifty-story office building. Underground, a vast two-level shopping center forms a city of its own, with stores, restaurants, amusements, and record shops; virtually everything one might want to buy or do during a lunch-hour walk is available.

By night, Lukhetho returns to the black world of Soweto, where thugs roam the streets on payday. "I have to adjust to these two worlds. I stay in Soweto, I work in Egoli—we call it gold city—Johannesburg. At first I didn't think I would ever get used to it. Just mixing with whites is different. What they do, their general interests are not the same as mine. Whites have a lot of jokes—some of their jokes I don't understand and I don't see

anything to laugh at." This isn't a language problem, but a vast difference in culture and experience. Lukhetho is fluent in English, Zulu, Sotho, and Swazi. He can get by in Afrikaans, but he prefers not to speak it.

"If you have to mix with people, you have to live in their world and they have to live in your world. So that was why I decided to myself, 'See what kind of people these are. See how they do things.' I used to watch the whites. I would introduce myself and say, 'This is who I am and what I do.' I would exchange a few words with them, then watch them, to see how they do things. The first few weeks, it was discouraging. I felt confused, inferior. I used to think about my qualifications and their qualifications. They have more schooling. Most of them have degrees. I preferred to watch them and hear what kinds of conversations they were involved in, because I knew that I was just a matriculant, and that worried me."

But it didn't hold him back. Within a year, Lukhetho's salary had increased from R170 to R400 ($195–$460) a month. This salary far surpasses that of most blacks and is more than some white clerks make. His temporary position became permanent; he became a computer programmer. Today he routinely takes a problem and works it out on the computer, bringing the completed program to his supervisor. His rapid rise in salary reflects his transition from trainee to skilled operator. Future salary increases will be small now.

"This bank—I can't say the name, but it's one of the biggest English banks in South Africa—wants to know exactly how much money it has out on loan, how much is due, and the equivalent amounts in different currencies. So I worked out a program for them. Now, all the bank has to do is tie into our computer from their own office to get all the information they need."

The world of Soweto that Lukhetho returns to at night is far less sophisticated. "When we first moved there, our house had no electricity. Dad had to fight to get it for us. My dad was an announcer for SABC, on Radio Bantu, for the Zulu service. He was there for sixteen years." In South Africa, all the media are operated by the government's broadcasting service. No independent stations exist. As one of the most popular Zulu broadcasters, Lukhetho's father reached millions of South African blacks. But as far as WRAB was concerned, he was just another Zulu, living in a matchbox house in Soweto. "In all that time, he only became an assistant to a white guy in the Zulu services. He couldn't go any higher. And he was only making R500 a month. The only reason we got a telephone was because the station had to be able to reach him." The phone is not a private instrument, as it is in the Western world and in Johannesburg. Anyone calling the Buthelezi household has to call through the Orlando switchboard and be connected to the house, as if it were a room in a hotel. But it is a privilege to have a telephone in Soweto, which has only a thousand phones for its one and a half million people.

Recently, Lukhetho's parents moved 150 miles away, from Soweto to Welkom, the center of South Africa's mining area, where his father is now the urban representative for Inkatha, the black cultural movement. He is a kind of ambassador for Chief Gatsha Buthelezi. That their family name is the same is a coincidence; the Buthelezis are the largest clan of all the

Zulus. Lukhetho's pride in his father's achievement is tinged with sadness. "My younger brothers and sisters will all move to Welkom in January, when the new school year starts. And that will leave just myself and my brother Norbert and his wife here in Soweto. My dad was known to many people through his radio work, but now he can work directly with people. That's one of the reasons he took the job. The salary was the other part. He had to make more money because of the children. My mother is a teacher and she has been able to get a job in Welkom."

Just a few weeks after his parents left for Welkom, Lukhetho was attacked in Soweto by *tsotsis*, the black thugs who prey on their own people. They attack mostly on Friday nights, when many people are paid. The *tsotsis* are partly a result of the very high unemployment among black youths. "They attacked me on a Friday night, about three weeks ago. I had worked late at IBM and I was going home about nine o'clock. As I walked across an open space near my house, where there's a bar and a burned-out post office and a soccer field, all of a sudden I saw three guys with knives. I moved back. They wanted money and I told them, 'I don't have any money.' One of them attacked me, he wanted to stab me. I punched him. Then another was attacking me, but they are weaker than me because they don't eat much and they drink a lot. As I punched one, he bit me on the cheek."

The wound has healed, but the crescent-shaped scar shows as a dark stain on his face. It will remain as a reminder of that night. "As one was coming, I kicked him and then punched the other again and pushed him toward the third. And then I was able to run to my house. A lot of people carry a handful of one-cent pieces, and when these guys try to rob them, they throw the coins at them. Then while the *tsotsis* are busy trying to pick them up, they run."

When his parents moved to Welkom, they took the family piano with them, a big loss for Lukhetho. "I had taught myself how to play. When I went away to school, I knew one tune: *Let It Be*, by the Beatles. Then last year I started hearing my own tunes in my head and I could work them out on the piano." Now he uses the piano at the home of friends who are well-known local musicians. Daughter Julie, a professional singer and pianist, has been giving Lukhetho some theory lessons, to bolster his natural

abilities. Rich melodies pour from his fingertips as he launches into a heartfelt rendition of some of his own songs. Julie tapes the best of the songs, to try to interest a local record company in recording them. Right now Lukhetho sees it as a hobby: "Music is for pleasure, not for making money." Still, if someone offers him the chance to record, he'd be delighted.

Much of his free time now is devoted to Inkatha. "The Inkatha Youth Brigade started about six months after Inkatha itself, in 1975. Chief Gatsha came to our school in Mpageni [KwaZulu] and talked to us. A group of us at school decided to take up membership, to be involved with community projects. We wanted to improve ourselves—the girls to learn how to sew, the boys how to garden—so that we can improve our homes and neighborhoods. Dad had been in Inkatha since it started and I joined on my own. But when I got back to Soweto, I decided to start a chapter of the Youth Brigade there because there were no young people in the movement. I didn't think I would ever succeed with the Youth Brigade because a lot of people don't like Inkatha, they don't like Chief Gatsha. They don't think he will succeed because he doesn't believe in violence.

"What we want is freedom. What we want is the unity of the black man. Chief Gatsha is my leader, not only as a Zulu but also as a black man. I feel with his leadership we are going to get there. He needs us to help him, to be able to unite more than 150,000 Inkatha members. Although the majority of Inkatha members are Zulus, there are also many Sothos, Xhosas, Shangaans, and Tswanas."

The youngest people attracted to the Inkatha Youth Brigade enjoy cultural activities like the traditional Gum Boot Bhaca—the dance Lukhetho teaches them on Saturday afternoons in the garage of his house. One boy beats out rhythms on a drum while Lukhetho throws his energies into the dance created by his Zulu forebears when they worked in the sugarcane fields in KwaZulu. The gum boots he and the children wear were worn by the black laborers who gradually replaced the Indians originally brought over to work in the muddy sugarcane fields.

Instead of separate development, Lukhetho sees blacks and whites living in the same world, a shared one, where blacks are not condemned to a homeland they do not know. "This is our world now. I have never been

to a kraal [family compound] though my father grew up in one, in KwaZulu. He was a herdboy until he went to school, when he was twelve. He became a teacher, but he's still battling to get his B.A. degree. He's doing a correspondence course at UNISA, in anthropology." UNISA (University of South Africa) is a university without a campus. All the work is done by correspondence. Lukhetho's mother also did a course at

UNISA, and he will probably follow in both his parents' footsteps. "I would like to go back to school next year, as a full-time university student, but I just can't afford it." It took Lukhetho's mother ten years to earn her B.A., but he is undaunted by the prospect of such a long stretch. He believes firmly that by educating themselves and proving their abilities, blacks can earn their freedom in South Africa.

Lukhetho can never escape his black skin, and that is central to the government's scheme of separate development. After Mozambique and Angola achieved independence, South Africa was flooded with Portuguese refugees. By the hundreds of thousands they have streamed into the country. Unlike Lukhetho, they were not born in South Africa, nor were their parents or grandparents or great-grandparents born in South Africa. But they are white. Five years after they arrive, they are entitled to become citizens and vote. They can live anywhere the whites live; they can own businesses and get licenses to have restaurants and sell liquor. Lukhetho cannot do any of those things, because he is black. "It is a killing thought," he says, his eyes filling with tears. "This person has been here a few years, yet he can own businesses, he can live anywhere. And I, a lifelong South African, born and bred here, cannot do a thing. I am not allowed to have even a small business in town, the white government wouldn't allow me to do that in South Africa. It is a killing thought." Even when he spoke of the deaths and destruction in Soweto, his emotions did not surface so painfully.

Lukhetho's girlfriend, Manono, who is training to be a nurse and whose contact with whites is limited to the doctors she works with, shares his pain, but disagrees on how to gain freedom for the blacks. She talked over her ideas with him in a multi-racial nightclub, one of several that existed briefly in Johannesburg before the police cracked down on them for serving liquor and allowing dancing among mixed groups. But for this one night, in Club New York City, Manono and Lukhetho experience what a mixed society could be like.

"I don't believe in Inkatha or in Chief Gatsha Buthelezi," Manono says. "We believe that there has been too much talking. Where has it gotten us? There must be blood spilled before we get our revolution. We can only get our freedom through violence."

Lukhetho disagrees. "They don't involve themselves, these people who speak of violence. It's not their blood they talk about. With violence, where would we end up? We would have to start from scratch. If everything was destroyed, where would we be?"

Four

Kathy Boraine

English-speaker

Aт an age when most South African white girls concern themselves only with exams, their appearance, and boyfriends, Kathy Boraine finds herself out of the mainstream. Her thinking puts her in opposition to most of her country's policies, and to her classmates and friends as well. But that is the way it has always been in the Boraine household, and that suits Kathy's own independent spirit. "I remember when I was in junior school, we had some black people staying with us and some of my friends were totally disgusted at the idea. But I've never made a line between the blacks and us. We've always had black friends in our lives. And even before Dad was in Parliament, he always had some kind of political involvement; he's always been very outspoken on political things."

Her father, Dr. Alex Boraine, a member of the liberal Progressive Federal Party, was elected to the South African Parliament in opposition to the government, so Kathy comes by her liberalism naturally. But her acceptance of it comes from her own convictions. "In school, we're not allowed to talk politics at all. We have no political organizations, and we're not allowed to have any political involvement, which is kind of silly for me, with Dad being in Parliament. During the last election, some of my friends asked me for Dad's bumper stickers for their cars, so I brought a few to school to give to them. And one girl said, 'You're not supposed to hand those out at school, you're not allowed to politic in school.' And she turned around and didn't talk to me again. It's a very stilted sort of atmosphere, so unnatural."

Kathy readily acknowledges that the fault lies in the system. "It's so hard to break the barrier of communication with the other races because of the way we live—everything is so segregated. But most of the kids are ignorant of what's going on around them. They're biased because they don't know anything else. They're too involved with themselves, with preserving their superior position as whites. And they actually believe that these people of other races have a lower intelligence rating. I try to argue with them, but it's no use at all."

Because of her beliefs, it was inevitable that Kathy would be enraged when she found that apathy was the general reaction to the news that black-consciousness leader Steve Biko had died at the hands of the police, while being held in detention.

"Nobody reacted at school, they couldn't be bothered. It didn't have any impact on the school as a whole. I was so upset that I decided to get some speakers to come to school. I invited Francis Wilson, who is a lecturer in sociology at the University of Cape Town, to come and talk to us." He came on October 19, 1977, a month after Biko's death, when a number of prominent people were banned, including Donald Woods and the Reverend Theo Kotze. "Francis edits a liberal magazine called *Outlook* —it was one of the few that wasn't banned. He was actually very good friends with all of these people. We asked him to come and he said, 'I'm just going to give a personal account of my knowledge of these people, just to get across that what the government said wasn't true, that they're not agitators or terrible people.' " Wilson came to school and afterward Kathy was upbraided for the talk. "People at school said, 'How can you have someone like this come and talk to us?' And we were told not to have people like that again. People just don't want to know what's going on around them."

Once a year, however, politics at school becomes mandatory. That's when the senior class takes a trip into town to see a session of Parliament. Naturally, the students turned to Kathy to make the arrangements for them. It was not her first visit. "Last year I went to Parliament when my Dad was giving a speech. And after the speech, Kruger, the Minister of Justice, stood up and slammed him, just slammed him for about half an hour, absolutely into the ground. 'We've got a file on you and we're going to get you,' he screamed. Oh, it was awful, seeing that and realizing that you can't do anything about it—it's a brick wall you're up against. They're in the majority and the opposition doesn't seem to get much changed at all.

"Some of us tried to get in touch with the young blacks from the townships. A few of us from school even formed an organization where we tried to arrange things we could do together, but it's too difficult because you can't go anywhere with blacks, any public place. You can bring them to your home, but they live so far away, it's impossible. And you can't go out there, because it's just too far to go out at night and then to come back."

The distances Kathy talks of aren't great. Her home in the white suburb of Pinelands lies a few miles from the heart of Cape Town, the most attractive city in South Africa. Situated on the Cape peninsula, the city is bounded by mountains on one side and the Atlantic Ocean on the other. The beautiful Table Mountain, with its cloud cover, forms the backdrop for the city and harbor. The black townships and the black squatter camps are only a few miles in the other direction from Kathy's home, but public transportation to the black areas is for blacks and is very inadequate, especially at night.

"There are always crises at the squatter camps where the black people live, because they don't have a legal right to live here in the Cape with their families. So they have these tin shacks and then the shacks are demolished—the authorities just bulldoze them—and the people have no place to go. The last time it happened, we filled up our car with bread and food and we went all the way out to where the camp had been. It was the most terrible sight to see the people in those ruins. There were no shops around, they haven't got any money, and you feel even worse just going around handing out this stuff, but what will happen to them otherwise? You feel so paternalistic, and the blacks your own age, they say, 'Oh, whitey,

whitey, you've got so much anyway.' They'll take it from you because they need it desperately, but it's too awful for words. We try—we don't know what to do about it."

Although Kathy was frustrated in her efforts to help the young blacks of the Cape, she was able to lend a hand in her father's reelection campaign. On September 20, 1977, South African Prime Minister John Vorster called for elections, to be held just ten weeks later, on November 30, even though his term had another eighteen months to run. In the parliamentary system, elections can be called at any time. The whole family, including two of Kathy's brothers, were involved in putting up posters, passing out pamphlets, and attending political meetings. "One night we were at a meeting in the Rondebosch town hall, which is next to Pinelands. It was just after Biko died. We were sitting on the wings of the stage and suddenly this thing—a tear-gas can—came in through the window. Dad was speaking. The can exploded on the floor—there was a big bang. People scattered on the floor, they were crying and breaking windows on the other side and trying to get out, to help the older people; and then it hit us on the stage. I thought I was going to die—your eyes swell up and you choke. We went out the back and called ambulances and tried to call the police. They took rather a long time to come. A lot of people were overcome by the smoke. My dad tried to get the people back into the meeting, as if to say, 'We're not going to let you break up our meeting just by doing this.' A lot of the people did come back and heard him through."

There were personal threats at home, too. "One night, just after Biko died, I was coming home from a dance at school, it was about half past nine, and I found a wreath at the door with a note attached to it. It said, 'You'll need one of these, too.' The threats were also coming in by letter— here and at Dad's office. One guy called and said, 'I'm going to shoot you while you're speaking tonight.' "

In addition to all this tension, and the tension that normally accompanies a political campaign, Kathy was in the midst of her year-end exams. "We were fetching people from the constituency who needed transportation to get to the polls. The cars were going out and I was coming home thinking, 'I'd better study for my math exam tomorrow.' I'd go back and have lunch where all the party people were working and I'd try to study there. After,

we'd get back to putting up the posters that people had torn down. After the polling station closed, I came home and had supper before we went to the town hall where all the results were coming in.

"We were getting more and more tense. Finally they were doing the actual count for Dad's district. At last someone came out to read the results, and there was so much noise, we couldn't hear the numbers. So we didn't really know who won until they said, 'Here is your MP for Pinelands,' and Dad came walking out! And it was such a relief, everyone was in tears; all the people who had been working there grabbed him and it really was exciting because I hadn't been here when he won his first election. I'd been in Johannesburg at school."

In spite of the energy she exerted to win the election, Kathy still wonders about the usefulness of the liberal voice in South Africa. "What he's doing in Parliament is to maintain a moderate line. I think it's worthwhile, I think someone has to keep up the only real legal opposition that has a voice, that can get into the newspaper. But the question is whether there's a role for the liberal white here; in fact, whether there's a role for the white at all. That's why the people in my age group are in such a dilemma."

That dilemma expresses itself in indecision. On Kathy's part, the indecision centers on whether she will go straight to the university after she takes her matric exams or will instead take a year off to try her hand at work. "I just really don't know. At one stage, I wanted to do journalism. I still would like to, but I think, oh, what's the future, and that's the whole problem. It's always in the back of your mind—is what I'm studying going to be worthwhile? Kids are not choosing certain professions, like law, because they wouldn't be able to use their training overseas. And a lot of my friends at school have left the country. I don't want to leave at all, but I just feel so uncertain.

"Living here, you do despair sometimes. There's the whole feeling of futility about our actions. I don't agree with war or anything like violence, and yet I think that must be easier to live with than feeling useless the whole time."

Kathy doesn't question the continued presence of whites in South

Africa. "How can four million whites just disappear? I don't think that's possible. There can be a revolution, sure. And if there is, I'm not concerned that I would have to leave the country. I could live here under black rule." But, right now, black rule seems a long way off. The present white rule, under the National Party, effectively keeps blacks from contributing to the decision-making process, or from forming groups to oppose the regime. At the same time, it moves to silence white opposition. This process takes many forms. Banning is one of them.

When several family friends such as the Reverend Kotze were banned, it became illegal for the families to get together. Her father still visits the Reverend Kotze, but Kathy says, "I don't go. I'd have to sit in another room if my father was talking to him. It's illegal for a banned person to see or talk to more than one person at a time. Unless you're banned or know someone who is, you can't understand the total implication of it on your life style. Theo Kotze phoned last night and asked for my father. And I said he'd gone out. There was a big party for my parents' twentieth anniversary at the Parliamentary Club last night, and I nearly said to him, 'Why, aren't you coming along?' Finally I gave him the phone number so he could call my parents at the party and wish them a happy anniversary." Just three months after that conversation, the Reverend Kotze escaped from South Africa. Donald Woods's dramatic escape made headlines, but the Reverend Kotze's manner of leaving remains unknown. He went quietly, out of despair, choosing to leave his country forever rather than live as a recluse, unable to fulfill his role as a minister.

The day after the party for her parents, Kathy was back in her school uniform. In South Africa, all students are required to wear uniforms. The uniform transforms Kathy from the near-adult who attended the party into a child. For Kathy, it's an unwelcome reminder of the government's control over so many phases of her life.

She wore the uniform one evening when she and her classmates served as waiters and waitresses at an annual event—a dinner given for the old people of her district. "It's an ongoing project for us. We visit them during the year at home and in old-age homes. We do their shopping and whatever else they need done for them. And then we have this big dinner and

entertainment for them. They look forward to it for such a long time." The teenagers rushed about, serving the old people in the school's meeting hall, then sat and chatted with them.

This school experience is quite different from the semester that Kathy spent in Boston, while her father attended a course in international affairs at Harvard. "I had a taste of the freedom Americans have and it was so hard for me to come back and settle down. It was so different, I couldn't believe it. The first day I went, they presented me with this whole book of subjects to choose from. We don't have a choice of subjects here. And no uniforms! It was so hard to fit back into the stilted atmosphere here where you can't express anything. There, you felt if you didn't understand something, you could go to your teacher and say, 'I'm having a problem.' Here you take extra lessons out of school if you don't understand. All you're trained for here is to pass the matric."

Kathy has other, less pleasant memories of America. "Their attitudes were really too liberal, it was very hard for me to fit in. And I would definitely not want to go to college there, as they call it. Everyone seemed to go, whether they had abilities or ambitions at all. They go because that's what you're supposed to do." On a less serious note, Kathy says, "I really hated the weather where we stayed—in Boston. It was so cold." As a South African, Kathy encountered instant hostility from some of her classmates in the United States, until she was given a chance to explain her own views of the government's racial policies.

In addition to the problems she and her family live with in South Africa, they are especially concerned about Zimbabwe Rhodesia, located on South Africa's northeast border, where until recently a small white minority ruled the black population. "My mom is from Rhodesia, and most of her family are still there. I went to school there, for a year, when my dad had gone back to Drew University in the States to do some advanced work. So my mother, brothers, and I stayed in a little farm town with my grandmother. My cousins were there, and I loved it. I went to a one-room school, just for the first four grades. My mother taught there for a while. We'd go running off after school and get a lift home in the back of a truck. Then we could go horse riding or go down to the river."

But the idyllic life whites lived in Zimbabwe Rhodesia has changed. A seven-year-long guerrilla war made most of the country unsafe, and forced the whites to accept elections leading to black majority rule. "My aunt and uncle have a farm just twenty miles from the Zambian border.

And they've found land mines on it. Luckily, the mines had been put in the wrong way, but they'd been traveling over them for three months. The farm next to them has been burned out, a man who lived next door has been killed. And everyone goes around with guns all the time. I'm petrified to go back there. I think my grandmother's all right, she has a friend who looks after her, but we're concerned about my uncle and aunt and their four little kids right on the border. But what can he do? He can't move his farm."

Adding to Kathy's fears are her boyfriend, Robin's. "A friend of Robin's, who went to school with him, was just killed on the border. It's so futile, to be killed on the South-West Africa border. Still, I don't want to leave the country. Even when I was in America, I missed the whole South African way of life, the climate, the people. I really did miss it. You only appreciate it when you go out of the country. I'd like to go and live out of the country for a while, but this will always be home for me."

With all the tensions around her, Kathy finds release in yoga. "I

started taking yoga classes when I was in America. Since I've been back, I haven't taken any more classes but every evening I spend at least half an hour on yoga, just before I go to bed. I'm so tense after sitting up and working, I find if I don't do it I can't go to sleep. I love to do yoga on the dunes. It's private; no one is around, and it's so quiet. I can only do that on the weekends, because we're not that close to the beach here. At the same time that I started practicing yoga, I found myself turning to vegetarianism. I would just eat meat on rare occasions. And then I found that I felt better if I didn't eat meat. Which is difficult here, because everyone here is mad for their *braai* [barbecue]. My father thinks I'm totally crazy. He cooks his *braai* and he gets so excited about it and his beautiful meat, but I say, ugh, no, I can't bear it. Mom's always been keen on vegetables, so I just have some vegetables and salads, and then I'll have cheese or make myself something with beans."

Kathy has stood up to her father on an issue far more serious than that of eating meat. When she was twelve years old, she stopped attending church services. "We were brought up to be very religious. My father is an ordained minister and past president of the Methodist Church. But I found the church people so hypocritical. Half of the people fell asleep during the sermon, the other half didn't care. They would go to cleanse themselves of their bad feelings, but none of them seemed to practice what they preached. In one Sunday school, they gave you a prize because you attended every Sunday of the year, not because of your dedication, and that seemed wrong to me. It's not the religion I've left, only the church. If I want to pray, I can do it in my room. I don't believe in separating people into Methodist, or something else. But I'm still a Christian. I do go to hear my father when he's preaching, but that's personal.

"I've met a lot of important people through Dad's work. It's been a big advantage for me, hearing the way different people think. It's helped me to understand the problems we face here. Dad often talks about things at home that he brings up in Parliament. Before the riots in Soweto, he talked about the situation there, pleading for something to be done. He warned about how frustrated the people were. Then when it happened, they said he was agitating for it to happen. And it just makes you feel more sickened

about the whole situation. You can see a thing coming, you can see it coming to a head, and Parliament carries on and says, 'No, we won't change anything.'

"That's why, everything we consider now in school, we have to say, 'What's the future in it? Is this something that will be worthwhile if I leave?' I don't want to leave at all. It's just so hard to commit yourself to something when you feel so uncertain about the future."

Five

Daniel Dewet Giliomee

Afrikaner

DANIEL DEWET GILIOMEE—familiarly known as Dewe—is an Afrikaans-speaking South African whose ancestors first arrived in 1735. Though his language derives from Dutch, the language spoken by the first whites who established themselves in the country, in 1652, many Afrikaners trace their ancestry to French or German forebears. Typical of his ancestors, Dewe grew up on a farm—a sheep farm on the edge of the Little Karoo, in the Cape Province. The Giliomees came to South Africa from France, but Dewe says, "None of us can speak French, though this is very much a French area. Most of the Afrikaners here have French ancestry. But there's no distinction among Afrikaners—French, German, Dutch—that's too long ago, it's all forgotten."

Until he was twelve years old, Dewe attended the little country school in the closest town, with twenty-seven other children from the surrounding farms. Then, like most rural South African whites, he was sent to a government-operated boarding school. But instead of going to a school where Afrikaans was the medium of instruction, Dewe travels seventy miles, to Rondebosch Boys High in Cape Town, where English is the language of instruction. His parents wanted him to have the advantage of speaking both official languages, English and Afrikaans, fluently. For Dewe, it was the start of a difficult and exciting venture into another world.

Like all South African students, Dewe had some English instruction in school. "But we really didn't learn to speak it at all. It was just a few hours a week; we spoke Afrikaans all the rest of the time." The farming community Dewe comes from is an Afrikaans-speaking world; there was no place to try out his few words of English. "My first day at Rondebosch was just a blank. I couldn't seem to remember a word of English. It's really different being taught English at school and then hearing everyone around you talking away. It sounds so fast when you hear English-speakers talking. Afrikaners don't speak English that fast even after they know it quite well. I just followed people around. There were three or four of my classmates who spoke Afrikaans and the guys were quite sympathetic. I could understand five or ten percent of the work in the first few weeks.

"I was afraid people would start laughing at me if I made mistakes. After about two months, I started trying to speak English. The boys

thought it was a fantastic challenge. As English-speakers, they said they would never have gone to an Afrikaans school. But I was very glad my parents sent me to English school. Even at twelve, I wanted to be able to speak English. I always got over 90 percent in my classes, and my parents thought I should be able to cope with the work." To be accepted into Rondebosch, Dewe had to show all-around abilities, in addition to high academic achievement. "You have to be interested in sports as well. If a boy has a good academic record, but doesn't do sports, the school would pass him by for another boy who didn't have quite as good a school record but who was good at sports. As it is, there are five hundred applications each year for about 125 places. Dad pays R130 [$150] each term for boarding—there are four terms a year." There is no fee for the schooling itself.

Class size for whites generally averages thirty students, although at Rondebosch classes range from twelve to twenty-four. Blacks attend classes of about fifty and must pay school fees. While most teachers in white schools are university-trained, only 14 percent of teachers in black schools have the equivalent of a high school diploma. For whites, everything is supplied, even the notebooks they write in.

Being the oldest of four boys, Dewe was the first in his family to go to Rondebosch. "My parents both speak English, although my mom speaks a lot better than Dad. She taught for a while in a school where there were a lot of English-speaking kids, so she got more used to speaking English with them. But my dad has always been a farmer and he really never has a chance to use his English." Although his parents wanted Dewe and his brothers to learn English, they didn't want him to pick up any mistakes, so they refrained from trying out their own English until he went to school.

From that rough beginning, Dewe progressed quickly. By the end of his first year, he could understand most of what was said, though he could not speak that well. In the next years at school, he continued to improve and soon his English was fluent, coming almost as naturally as his Afrikaans. In his last two years at Rondebosch, his English became polished. In his last year at Rondebosch, Dewe takes English on the highest level, with classwork as demanding as in his Afrikaans studies. Most students take the second language on a lower level, giving them an estimated 70 percent proficiency in the use of the language when they complete their studies.

As soon as Dewe started coming home for holidays, his parents began to speak English with him. The three younger boys now heard English being spoken and picked up a few words. By the time his brother Francois, three years younger, started at Rondebosch, he was much more familiar than Dewe had been with the sound of English, though he, too, could not speak it at first. When the youngest brother, now nine, goes to high school, he will have quite an advantage. "It was tough at the beginning," Dewe says. "I had a lot of catching up to do. But it's absolutely fantastic to be able to speak English and Afrikaans. Culturally, I am still more Afrikaans than English. But I am completely bilingual. I go to the Nico-Malan Theater to see Afrikaans drama, and I go to Maynardville [a suburb] to see Shakespeare. I love both. Now they've introduced Xhosa into some schools, too. My brother Altus is studying that in primary school, in addition to English and Afrikaans.

"I find that you can express some things better in Afrikaans. There are little words that describe a thing so exactly, you can't possibly get an English word that describes it in such a detailed way. But English is the international language. If you want to go into business, I think you need English, more than English people need Afrikaans."

So Dewe is looking for a future beyond the farm. "Say, for instance, that I don't want to come back to the *plaas*—the farm—after school," Dewe explains, "or maybe I can't come back to the farm. Dad thinks it can only support two of us four brothers. So at least two of us will have to work at something else. Dad came to farming when he was seventeen, just out of school. He didn't go to university. If something goes wrong with the farming, he can't do a thing. That's all he knows.

"Now my friends around the farm are jealous, I think they would like to have the same opportunity. I've mixed more with people. I've read a lot of English books. It's given me a more complete look at life, being bilingual. Somebody who lives an Afrikaans life, he won't know about those things I've discovered, so he wouldn't feel he's missing things. But once he has discovered them, he'll realize that learning English has been an advantage."

For Dewe, speaking both languages is more than a social grace. "I plan to go to Stellenbosch University after I do my National Service. Although Afrikaans is the language of instruction, the textbooks are in English." As a written language, Afrikaans is still in its infancy, compared with the volume of material available in English. Textbooks, particularly in the sciences, lag behind the demand, so many students at Afrikaans-medium universities like Stellenbosch are taught in Afrikaans, but study from English textbooks.

Before he set out for boarding school, Dewe's life revolved around the family's 3,000-acre farm and its 2,000 Merino sheep, the type that is famous for the luxurious wool it produces. These sheep can be traced back to 1789 when a pair of the prized animals were presented by the Spanish king to the Dutch. "This particular farming area is the best for raising Merinos. The climate is perfect for them, so the wool is the best quality. We grow wheat here, too, in addition to having the sheep. We put in lucerne—a kind of clover—with the wheat. Then when we harvest the wheat, the lucerne is left in the ground. That's the main food that the sheep graze on here. We couldn't do without it. So the grazing and the sheep fit together."

There are fewer Afrikaners farming the land each year. Forty years ago, half the Afrikaner population were farmers. Today the ratio has dropped to 20 percent. The farming Afrikaner, narrowly set in his ways, is slowly giving way to the more liberal kind of family, like the Giliomees. But the typical figure still exists. "In the Transvaal, you get the real Afrikaner," Dewe explains, heavily exaggerating his pronunciation of "Afrikaner," dragging out the "a" sound. "You know—the real Voortrekker. We're not the Transvaal type of fanatical Afrikaner. I don't think we'd fit in easily with those people. I myself enjoy the city, the social life of Cape Town. But I readjust easily. Today I'm on the farm, tomorrow I'll be back at school. It takes me about a day to get into the rhythm of Cape Town. Then I come back here and I get into the rhythm of farm life again."

Afrikaners are very literal with their place names. The farm that Dewe's father inherited from his father is called Voorschiet—Afrikaans for "mortgage." The town itself, which consists basically of a post office, a shop, and grain silos, is called Protem, a Latin word meaning "for the time being." "This is where the railroad ended," Dewe explains. "It was supposed to be expanded, but it never was, so this remains the end of the line." And the name the railway prospectors put on their survey maps remained also.

While Dewe was growing up, farm life was restricted to the home. The distances between farms and communities meant that any trip had to be for a very specific purpose. "We didn't even go to church every Sunday. We belong to the Ned Geref Kerk [the Dutch Reformed Church attended by the majority of Afrikaners]; it's thirty-two kilometers [about fifteen miles] each way to the church, so we would go every second or third Sunday." Before each meal at home, the family offers a prayer. At Rondebosch High School, church attendance is compulsory every Sunday.

As Dewe tussles with a ram weighing about two hundred pounds, he says, "I was two or three years old when I started with the sheep. One of the first memories I have is seeing the lambs born. At lambing time, there will be about a thousand lambs born within a few weeks. I like it very much. It's hard work, but it's very rewarding. During this school holiday, we dosed just about all the sheep on the farm, vaccinating them against worms. I used to help out when I was little, I'd hold the bottle while Dad injected the serum. I didn't know how to do it, so I'd just be handing things, and holding the sheep and watching. Now I do it myself. We've got a chute-system passage and we move all the sheep through it in two and a half days. It's quite tough. You have to keep the sheep still, then push the needle in on the side of the ear, just under the jaw."

It's a long, hard day when they're out working with the sheep. "This past Friday, I had to dose five hundred sheep, feed them and check them. I got up at six o'clock, to put out bales of straw and mealies [corn]. I started dosing at nine o'clock and worked until three o'clock in the afternoon, finishing those five hundred before we had some lunch. It was raining from one till three, so we were working in the pouring rain. Then we milked our cows, working until it was dark.

"We have four or five Coloureds working on the farm; we don't have Bantu. We prefer the Bantu to work with the animals, they love animals, and they're good with them. But this is a Coloured area, and if you want to have Bantu, you have to go to the Transkei to fetch them." The difficulty

facing Dewe and his father stems from the fact that the Cape is a "Coloured labor preference area" (so designated by the government). The Coloureds have always stayed close to their roots in the Cape. In order to force employers to hire Coloured labor, in 1966 the government froze the number of blacks permitted to work there, and denied them the right to have their families with them. But Coloureds traditionally have not been farm workers, so when Dewe's father wanted blacks, he had to bring them in from Transkei, where there is a surplus of black labor.

"You can't go to a township near here because those Bantu don't want to work on the farm. They're from the city. After a week, they would just go back to the city. But if you go to the Transkei, where they grew up on farms, they know what it's like. We had one working here for fourteen years. He had his family here. But that was before the law was declared. As soon as the law was made, his family had to go back, and that's why we lost him. Many Bantu want to come here, because there aren't any jobs in the Transkei, even if it means being without their families. Our Coloured boys who work here stay here with their families and their kids; everybody's here. And that's okay because this is where the Coloureds are from, this is their country."

South African whites call their servants "boys" no matter what their age. It's a holdover from the days when blacks were thought of as children, needing whites to look after them. This paternalistic attitude exists today, even though blacks are slowly being permitted to enter the business world, slowly allowed to get more education.

As Dewe prepares to go out with his father to inspect the sheep, the sheep dog waits in his pen, excitedly pacing back and forth. Dewe releases the dog, and off they go. Out in one of the grazing areas, the dog is put through his paces. He wriggles under the fence and barks at the hundreds of sheep in the meadow. In a minute, he has them all herded in the right direction.

Driving across the gently rolling hills of the farm, Dewe points out a herd of fifty springbok. "We keep them just for the pleasure of looking at them. Father investigated the idea of opening a game park on our land, then decided against it. But we keep the springbok anyway." The springbok, a gazelle, is South Africa's national symbol. Versions of it appear on every-

thing from the national airline to the blazers of its sports champions.

The day before, a trap had been set for a lynx which had killed one of the big springbok. "There are fewer wild rabbits now, so the lynx will go for the springbok or for the sheep. I don't think we have caught him yet." When he came to the trap, Dewe was surprised to find the lynx in it, snarling and hissing as he approached. The rabbit which had been used for bait was lying in the cage. The lynx had killed it but had not eaten it after the trap was sprung. Dewe returned to the house and got his .22 and some ammunition. His brothers and some visiting cousins and friends all piled into the back of the panel truck to watch him shoot the lynx.

He took their sheep dog as well, to see if it could find the lynx by its scent. The whole operation was a series of lessons. Dewe kept in mind his responsibility to his younger brothers and cousins, the dog was to learn something about wild animals, and everyone had a look at an animal that was killing off some of the farm's precious livestock. After making sure that everyone was standing well behind him, Dewe took careful aim and shot the lynx in the trap. His brother Francois tested the lynx, prodding it with a twig until there was no response. Once the lynx was taken out of the trap, all the children took a good look at it, without making much fuss.

Driving back, Dewe said, "City boys would have reacted differently to the shooting. On a farm, you accept these things. If an animal kills your animals, it has to be killed. I grew up with a gun. It's very usual on a farm. I had a gun when I was seven years old. I like to shoot—guinea fowl, pheasants. We even have a clay-pigeon machine on the farm, and I used to practice shooting with that. I know you could drop me anywhere in Africa and I could take care of myself. I could live off the land."

This self-confidence pervades Dewe's school life, too, and he easily enters into classroom discussions. Looking very different in his school uniform—consisting of a blazer, flannel trousers, a white shirt, and a striped tie—Dewe attended classes in math, family relationships, and history. Student participation was stressed in each.

Just a five-minute walk from Rondebosch is Rustenburg High, the white girls' school. The two schools take turns holding dances and other events. With chaperones from both schools looking on, Dewe and his class-

mates enjoyed an evening's "disco" dancing in the meeting hall at Rustenburg.

Dewe enjoys a variety of sports, including cricket, tennis, and squash, but his main interest is rugby. On the vast fields that spread out from the main classroom and dormitory buildings, Dewe and his classmates practice blocking and tackling. All around them, other teams practice their sports, all under the supervision of teachers. Sports activities are carefully structured and disciplined, even more so than some of the classes.

On Tuesdays, Dewe finishes his classes for the day and hurries out to another field, where he gathers together the younger boys for their weekly Cadets session. For fifty minutes, the children march back and forth while Dewe, who is a Cadets sergeant, and two other final-year students give commands. "It's very good for them, it gives them some idea of discipline. When they have to do their National Service, they'll be ready. All the schools do it." All the white schools, that is. For now, military service is mandatory only for whites. "There are films and lectures on at the same time as the Cadets are training that the other boys in my grade go to. But I don't mind missing them. I think it's worthwhile doing this."

Just before the end of his final year at Rondebosch, Dewe received his

National Service notice. He had to complete the form, advising the government whether he intended to go on to university immediately or do his two years of National Service first. "Whenever I go into service, I'll still have to do my border duty. Even if I do university first and serve four years from now, there will still be troops at some border. If it's not the Namibia border, then it will be the South Africa border. The troops will still be there, make no mistake. Things won't clear up so easily." This continued uncertainty is particularly on the minds of the white English-speakers. In his English-medium school, Dewe hears a lot about the question of holding British passports. "I would say that two out of every ten have British passports. Some English-speakers are really South Africans, but I think some of them don't really care about the country. I think, military-wise, the Afrikaans people are holding this country together.

"I follow politics, but for now I don't want to get involved. I don't think I will vote, because I don't think I know enough yet to cast a vote."

Almost casually, he talks of discarding a privilege that blacks can only dream of having. "I'd rather stay out of voting than vote for somebody or some party that I don't even know about."

Though his political views are still largely unformed, Dewe represents the Afrikaner of the future, the Anglicized Afrikaner; totally bilingual and at home in either culture. He comes from the farming past of the country, but has his eye on its economic future. It is people like Dewe who may form the bridge over what is, even today, a truly formidable chasm between the two white groups of South Africa. But his bilingualism and biculturalism do not begin to bridge the far more dangerous separation between white and black.

Six

Nombulelo
Princess Fuma

Crossroads Xhosa

CROSSROADS APPEARS, full-blown, as one drives along Klipfontein Road. One moment there is just desolation; the next, densely packed tin shacks, lining the road and stretching out as far as the eye can see. It's a tightly built mass, crisscrossed by footpaths and sandy roads. Many people have automobiles, late models in good order. The tin shacks have proper doors, with locks, and windows with glass panes. Some have little gardens where vegetables grow in the sandy soil. Some have flowers growing around the fences. One has a tiny duplicate tin shack in the yard, for the family dog.

The children are clean, well dressed, and have the bright eyes that reflect good health. Chickens wander about freely, as do a few dogs. Women and girls of all ages walk by, balancing heavy pails of water on their heads. Everyone passes by with a smile and a greeting. Cars drive by slowly, mindful of the children and the dust that they raise. Trucks make deliveries to the many businesses that keep the community going.

Nombulelo Fuma, a Xhosa girl who prefers to use her Christian name, Princess, lives in Crossroads. Bright and cheerful, well groomed and neatly dressed, she studies at night to learn English and looks after her younger brothers and sisters while her parents are working. Many threads of the racial fabric of South Africa are woven together in her complex story, which is echoed in the lives of hundreds of thousands of blacks.

As a Xhosa, Princess is deemed by the South African government to be a resident of Transkei, a homeland that was given its independence in 1976. No other nation in the world has recognized this independence, so Transkei remains an appendage to South Africa in every sense. Princess was born in Cape Town, but it is illegal for her to live there. Her parents came to Cape Town in 1958, looking for work. "My parents did not have land to plow in Transkei. There is no work there. There is no food there. That is why they came." But those reasons do not suffice, in the eyes of the law. The desire to work conflicts with the policy of separate development. Blacks are to develop in their own areas, and specifically in their own homelands. Because there are so many Coloureds in the Cape, the government designated the area as a "Coloured labor preference area." For twenty years, one of the government's hopes has been to reduce the number of blacks in the Cape. That hope is constantly thwarted, for the number has risen steadily, though blacks without work contracts cannot legally remain in the Cape. Even if a man is legally working, his wife and children may not come to live with him. They must remain in the homeland.

Princess's father does not have a work contract. "When my father came here, he worked as a casual worker. He was a garden boy, going from there to there. He worked in private houses. When I was born, my father was doing roadwork with the Council. Now he empties the dustbins [garbage cans] for the Council, here in Crossroads." Here, then, is a family living in Crossroads, with a father who is earning his living as a legal employee of the Divisional Council of the Cape. The Council is the local governmental body in this section of the Cape province, and it is this agency that is determined that these people will not be allowed to stay in the camp. Although he is a married man, Princess's father is supposed to stay in the single men's hostel, the only place where legally employed black men can live. Because he doesn't want to live apart from his family, he lives in Crossroads. His only crime is the wish to live with his wife and his children.

When Princess's parents left Transkei twenty years ago, they never looked back. Its recent "independence" makes no difference to them, because it didn't produce the jobs they needed. When they piled their belongings together and climbed into a small pickup truck to start the long, slow journey to Cape Town, they were not alone. Other families joined them, following a well-worn path taken by many Xhosas from Transkei. In its shiftings about in Cape Town, Princess's family has always been surrounded by Xhosas.

Before 1975, Crossroads did not exist. At that time, the more than twenty thousand people who live here were scattered throughout the area. Like so many of them, Princess and her family were often on the move, living in makeshift homes. They did not qualify to live as a family in one of several legal black townships, such as Guguletu, which is within walking distance of Crossroads. There are many more squatters than the twenty thousand in Crossroads. An estimated two hundred thousand are at the Cape. And the numbers increase, in spite of the government's plan to restrict black workers by denying them the right to live with their families. Instead of separating, the families keep on the move, trying to stay out of the way of the authorities. From time to time, the police would come and tell the people they must go. They used bulldozers to knock down their shacks. But the people would retreat farther into the bushes and build other shacks.

In 1975, Princess and her family were told to move to the area now known as Crossroads. "The white people—the Council's inspectors—told us all to go there. We came from Grassy Plains, from Brown's Camp, from all over the area. Squatters—people living in shacks—were told to come here. It was just bushes then, and there were snakes here, big snakes, cobras. The men killed them with sticks, but even now there are still some snakes here."

As she talks, Princess's voice is drowned out by a jet passing overhead. It is so low, the individual windows can be made out. Crossroads is on the flight path for planes taking off from D. F. Malan, Cape Town's major airport. The noise stops conversation completely, and often.

Crossroads gets its name from two major roads that intersect at the point where the community begins. All ordinary habitation ends several miles off. This land is called the Cape Flats and is notorious for the winds that howl across it, blowing fine sand everywhere. A pervasive smell of the salts present in the sandy soil lies over the area, which was a wasteland before Crossroads sprang up. Title to the land is in dispute, lending a peculiar semi-legal status to the camp.

"When we were told to come here, we were staying not far away. So we just took our clothes out of the *ityotyombe*—the shack—and we knocked it down ourselves. We hired a van to move the zincs—the tin sheets—that we make the house with, and our clothes, and our furniture. And we came here, where Klipfontein Road meets Lansdowne Road. There were only a few houses then. So we saw that place where we built our house—it's #660. We saw that it was a nice place, with some trees. Some people had no trees, only bushes. And it was quite close to the road."

The community grew rapidly from those beginnings in 1975 as others heard that the Council itself was sending the squatters to this place. More and more families moved in and put up their tin shacks. Rough paths were kept, the width of an automobile.

But the basic illegality remained, and periodically the police would come through the camp, looking for those without passes. "When they come, they knock very hard. Bang, bang, bang. Then they open the door, they ask, 'Where is your mother, where is your father?' We say, 'They are gone, they ran away.' Because as soon as the police come, the people start to call out, they sing out, like this." Here Princess stands up and sings out the warning in Xhosa. "*Kubomyu!*" "And then, when you hear them, you must come out the door, you must look and call, 'Where are they?' And you pass along the warning. So they would come at night, sometimes at midnight, sometimes at one o'clock, two o'clock in the morning. And this time I was in bed when I heard a woman crying out the warning. And I got up and told my mother. She was fast asleep. I told her, 'The police are here.' Then my mother and father, they get up and take the blankets and wrap themselves up and they run away. They run into the bushes. And we children stayed in the house, because children don't need passes. And meanwhile, parents were running away, all over Crossroads. There were many police, with big vans. They had torches to shine in the houses."

Princess was just fifteen years old then. Many people were taken away in that raid, and in others that followed. Children were left behind; those

who went to jail knew that the community would care for the children. Sometimes the children did not know if their parents would be back that same day, or not for three months—the term of imprisonment imposed if they could not meet the thirty-rand fine ($34.50). "That time I became very worried, because my parents were gone for so long. Some of the neighbors had already come back, but still my parents were out. And I was frightened. I didn't know if they were arrested. It was morning when they finally came back. I was so relieved."

The raids continued intermittently until July 1976, when Crossroads was declared an emergency camp, giving it a quasi-legal status. The Council then began to provide the most basic sanitary services, installing water taps at locations along the two main roads that border Crossroads, and providing for trash pickup and the emptying of buckets used in the outhouses. For these services, each household was charged R7 a month. The Council became the landlord of Crossroads.

"We pay R7 a month to stay here, but we built our house ourselves. My father built it. We had our zincs, the sheets we use for the walls, that my father bought from the scrap yard. It took two days to put the walls up and the wood supports and the roof. Then my mother did the inside. She put up papers to cover the walls, to keep out the wind. And the floor she made of wood, and covered it with linoleum. That took another day."

Inside, the house is neat and clean. Two bedrooms have been partitioned off from the central space where the family eats. The parents have one bedroom; the children share the other. Light comes from gas lamps, and cooking is done on a paraffin stove. When Crossroads was declared an emergency camp, many families felt they had a permanent home and they bought furniture for the first time. They have made real homes of those tin shacks. But wood, paper, and zinc don't provide much protection when winter begins. "When it's raining, it's leaking. The rain comes up underneath, and onto the floor. And the wind blows the dust in. When it's really windy, the home is shaking. Sometimes the sheets of zinc are taken off by the wind. And there are rats. They come at night, you hear them, they even go over our faces, they bite us. And then we just wake up and we sit, we don't sleep again. We do buy rat poison, but they don't all die.

"It's hard to live here. We must carry the water from the road. We do catch cold in the wintertime. We light our tins and we make a fire in the house. But we don't care about the place, the only thing we are concerned about is work. And my father has always found work here."

After Crossroads was declared an emergency camp, the raids stopped, but Princess's mother was still in the Cape illegally. And one day she was caught. "In 1977, they arrested me in Langa [a nearby black township] with my mother while we were eye-shopping [window-shopping]. She didn't have a pass. I told them, 'I am too young.' Still, they put us in the van. I said to them, 'You are wasting your time, they are going to let me free, I am too young to carry a pass.' My mother was really sad. She even said to me, 'Stop it, keep quiet,' but I never stopped. They took me to jail. Then they let me go because I was young. I left my mother sitting there on the benches, crying. When I saw my mother crying, I began to cry." It was up to Princess to take the bus home and get money from her father to bail her mother out. He borrowed money from different people to pay the fine. This time it was R50 ($57.50), more than her father earns in a week.

If the people of Crossroads were uncertain about their status, so were the authorities, who, for a while, tried to maintain some control by doing surveys and numbering the shacks. "The first numbers we had were yellow. The social workers would come and ask many questions. And the next day men would come with a van, put your clothes in the van, and take you to the railroad station. Then they went back and demolished the house with a bulldozer. I was lucky, they didn't demolish my house. I don't understand why they do these things to us." The authorities would order people out, give them tickets to go back to the Transkei, and put them on the trains. "But instead of going seven hundred miles, they would just get off at Belleville [the next stop]. Then they would come back and build their houses again. At that time, the inspectors were foolish enough not to take the materials.

"If the inspectors from BAAB [Bantu Affairs Administration Board, now called Plural Relations] came and did a survey, and they saw a house without a number, they just put a number on it." And so it went, through the second phase, the red numbers. Then came the third phase: the houses were given numbers in white paint. And when the numbering was finished, Crossroads was finished growing. The order went out—no more houses were to be built. In less than three years, Crossroads had grown into a city of three thousand houses and an estimated twenty thousand people. It became a community with *shebeens* (bars), venders selling meat and vegetables, repair shops—in fact, someone to provide almost every kind of service required by a town of its size. And two schools were built, with funds from social-service groups and foundations.

When Princess and her best friend, Joyce, each have fifty cents, they walk down the road to the "Chinese store," so called because it is run by a Chinese family. The store is the message center of Crossroads, a place to make a telephone call, a place to get mail. And on Friday and Saturday nights, movies are shown there. Karate films rate high on the list of favorites, since the action is easy to follow.

With all the moving around and living in squatter camps, Princess has only managed to complete six years of schooling. "I am trying to catch up now. I go to night school, four nights a week. We don't have school on Friday night, because it's too dangerous to be out. That's the night when the *skollies* [thugs] come, to steal the pay packets." Crossroads, with its own community patrol force, actually suffers from less crime than the official black townships just a few miles away. But crime does increase on Friday nights, along with drinking.

"I study at Noxola school [the name means "peace"] here in Crossroads, where the children take their classes during the day." Because there is no electricity anywhere in Crossroads, they study by gaslight and by candle-light. In a drafty, unheated room, people of all ages apply themselves to copying the lesson from the blackboard. Some put their babies to sleep on the wooden benches, rising from time to time to comfort a crying child. The light is very dim, the blackboard is very worn. But the hunger for education is stronger than the obstacles. "If you are not well educated, you have no job. The only thing I want is to finish my education." But even with an education, for Princess there is no legal work in the Cape. It's likely that she will become a maid, like her mother, a job that might enable her to get by without a permit, if she can avoid the police.

Education or no, when the authorities discover Princess, they will want to send her to Transkei, a homeland of the Xhosa. "I have never been in Transkei, I do not know Transkei." Not only is Princess ignorant of the land, but she is also ignorant of the Xhosa culture, the culture the government insists she is a member of. Xhosa tradition is rich in ritual: initiation rites for both boys and girls are strictly observed. To keep up these traditions, some people journey all the way back to Transkei, seven hundred miles away. But for most, the ritual has been lost in their urban environment. Princess has never seen or even heard of the *intonjena* ceremony, performed when a girl reaches puberty, to mark her passage into womanhood. Princess has made the passage without the ceremony.

Xhosas like Princess are coming to live as other black-township dwellers.

Today dress is Westernized and modern. In Crossroads, however, a few women still wear the Victorian-inspired clothes that date back to the time missionaries arrived in Transkei. They wear *isibentele*, the traditional turban that identifies a married woman.

Though dress and customs have changed, the tradition of *lobola* survives. This tradition cuts across tribal lines and is followed as strictly by a Zulu living in a kraal in KwaZulu as by a Swazi living in a tiny brick house in Soweto. And it holds for Princess, too. "Yes, I have a boyfriend here, but my parents don't know about him. His name is Aaron and he stays at #255. But it is tradition that my parents should not know about him, unless we want to become engaged. Then he must send his parents to talk to my parents." So, from one dusty part of Crossroads to another, Aaron's parents will come to *ityotyombe* #660, to arrange for the payment of *lobola*. "After his parents talk to my parents, they will come with the *lobola*, which will be about R800 [$920]. It should be ten oxen, but in Crossroads you can't give oxen, so you just give money. And the money goes to my parents. They buy everything we need for the house." Because of the amount involved,

some men pay out the *lobola* over many years, even long after the couple are married and have their own family.

While Princess's mother goes to work each day as a maid for a white family in Cape Town, Princess spends her day at home, taking care of her brothers and sisters, cleaning the house, and cooking. This routine was broken when the community staged a play, written by three residents of Crossroads. Called "What next shall I do because they ask for pass?" the play was first performed at the Noxola school. Then, to raise money to help the community in its battles in the courts, the play was performed at the Space Theater in Cape Town and in several of the more liberal and affluent white suburbs. Princess talks over the play with her neighbor Muriel, one of the authors. "I played a Xhosa girl, someone who had never been at school. And in the play the inspectors come and ask me about a pass. I

didn't know what this inspector means when he says, 'Vars your pass, you bloody kaffir?' I didn't even know what a kaffir is." Literally, "kaffir" means "unbeliever," but it has long been an obscene word when applied to blacks.

"It didn't matter that my English was not so good, because I spoke Xhosa in the play. We did the play to tell the white people how we feel about what is being done to us. Some of the whites in the audience didn't know other white people were acting like that to us. They were so embarrassed; I could see that, it was written on their faces." But symbolic protest seems to have little real effect. In the past, squatter camps have been demolished by the authorities. First a warning goes out to the squatters that they must move; then the bulldozers arrive and homes are flattened. Warning notices have started to appear in Crossroads.

These people have seen the bulldozers, they've seen tin shacks flattened in seconds. They live in the hope that this will not happen in Crossroads, because the white people sent them to live there. But Crossroads must come down, because it exists in defiance of the law. To the people who live there, it is better than life in Transkei, where children are doomed to a half life of malnutrition, where families without fathers live and wait for money that may never come. Living in Transkei, for these people, is worse than living in Crossroads and waiting for the bulldozers and the midnight knock on the door.

Seven

Symanthia Moodley

Indian girl

THE SOUTH AFRICAN government calls Symanthia Moodley Asian; she considers herself South African. The government says she must live in an area designated for Indians. She speaks no Indian language, though she was given the Indian name Krishna Devi, along with her Christian name, Symanthia. Her ancestors spoke Tamil, a language used in the region of southern India where her ancestors were from. Like the Coloureds, the Indians do not fit into South Africa's apartheid policy, the policy of separate development, for they have no claim to any homeland in South Africa, though 83 percent of them live in Natal.

Symanthia's great-grandparents were among the Indians brought to Natal, then a British colony, in 1860, to work as indentured laborers, in the sugarcane fields. The Tamils were among the poorest of the Indians and had the least to lose in making the frightening trip across the Indian Ocean to a continent they knew nothing of. They were brought in because the sugarcane farmers were unsuccessful in exploiting as laborers the abundant black population in Natal. But, by the end of the nineteenth century, the blacks were being forced to work in the fields to pay newly imposed taxes. The Indians, no longer needed in the fields and numbering more than two hundred thousand, became a problem in the eyes of the government, a problem that continued to grow. In 1926, the Union of South Africa made a belated and unsuccessful attempt to repatriate the Indians to India. Successive governments pursued the attempt until finally, on February 8, 1962, the Indians were declared legally permanent inhabitants of South Africa. Today more than 750,000 Indians live a second-class existence in South Africa, more privileged than the Coloureds and the blacks, but less privileged than the whites, always carefully kept in second place. They are the smallest recognized racial group in South Africa and are kept apart from the whites and other races by law.

Symanthia Moodley thinks of herself as a South African first, then as an Indian, but it is as an Indian that she is judged and kept separate. At seventeen, she knows just what she can and cannot do. And usually she keeps to her own kind, to avoid the hurt of racial prejudice. Symanthia lives in the heart of Durban, South Africa's biggest port, a modern metropolis in the province of Natal on the Indian Ocean. During the South African winter, mild by the standards of Europe and the northern United States, many come to Durban's beaches because the climate then is at its best: balmy, pleasant days and refreshingly cool evenings.

The city's hotels, some of them of the highest standard, line the shore; the bustling area of Indian shops and apartments is a five-minute drive away. Yet, only two years ago, Symanthia's father had to fight for his family's right to stay in the city, joining with many others to protest against a massive forced removal planned by the government. "This whole Indian area had been proclaimed white. More than seventy-five thousand of us were supposed to be moved from our homes, to some district out of town. They had already moved some of the Indians down in the market area to make way for a highway bypass. You can see the bypass—they haven't finished building it yet." For two years, Symanthia's father and their friends and neighbors battled to be allowed to stay in the area where they had lived all their lives. Finally they won, but in the meantime, apartments were neglected, houses became rundown. A sense of indecision hung over them; no one wanted to spend money on a house they might have to leave. "We

had actually given up hope, we had one foot out the door."

The knowledge that at any moment they could be told to move from their home to make way for whites started the family talking about leaving South Africa. "We have relatives who live in Toronto, in Canada, and they're happy there. They emigrated with their young daughters. Things weren't very good here for business then. But gradually things have improved. There aren't so many restrictions on us now. And I really didn't want to go. I was just about to start studying at the university."

Once the decision was made to stay, Symanthia's father decided to build a new house. "Our apartment is really too small with myself and my two sisters and my parents. We're all crammed in here, in these tiny bedrooms.

It's hard for me to find a quiet place to study with enough room for my books and papers. We started talking about building a house, but we didn't make the final decision until after August 20. That marks the end of a month-long period during which no important decisions are made. In our religion, it's considered an inauspicious time."

Though the Durban Indians won that battle, others have not been so fortunate. Pageview, a section of Johannesburg, was taken from the Indians. Five thousand families were moved, and all the Indian traders were moved out, to enable the white business district to expand. The Indians were moved to Lenasia, near Soweto. The white government chose a site and built a new shopping area for them called Oriental Plaza. But the contrived atmosphere doesn't duplicate the charm of the old area. The many whites who enjoyed the flavor of the old area don't bother making the trip to Oriental Plaza. But the Indian traders have to make the long trip to Johannesburg from Lenasia, fifteen miles away. They have no choice.

Symanthia and her family will feel more secure when they move to their new house, which is being built in the Indian area called Reservoir Hills. Partly because of the deterioration of their Durban neighborhood, youth gangs have moved in. Now Symanthia restricts her movements, never going out alone at night. Even for a group, there is danger. "One evening I was walking to the bioscope [movie house] with my sisters and some other girls in our building, and a cousin of mine, a boy, who came with us. We were crossing the street to the cinema and there was a fight going on between some of the boys from the area. This gang was watching for one boy, and they had knives. An African thought my cousin was part of the gang and actually came right towards him to stab him. He managed to escape in time. We just walked as fast as we could, away from there. We went into the bioscope, but I tell you, we were really shaken up. So it is dangerous. If they're fighting and you get into their way, you're going to get hurt as well.

"That night we were going to see an American movie. Sometimes we go to see Indian movies—there are four Indian bioscopes nearby. I don't understand the language, but if I'm with someone who can tell me the story, I enjoy watching it. All the bioscopes we go to are for non-whites." When Symanthia ventures out of the Indian area, she becomes very cautious. "I've never gone to a place where I was asked to leave because I was non-white. You see, we're used to asking before we enter a place. We find out before if we can go. Once, we had visitors from Johannesburg and we thought we'd take them to the rides at the beach front, the Fun Fair. I went up to the lady selling tickets and I asked her if Indians were allowed and she said we weren't. So we didn't go there."

Unlike buses in most of the cities in South Africa, buses in Durban are not segregated. But when Symanthia takes a bus to go to the beach-front area, barely ten minutes from where she lives, she knows she is entering the white world. "I feel more comfortable in the Indian section. When I travel by bus to the beach front, people stare at me. They turn around to look. And I feel it's a critical stare, as if they're wondering why I am in that place." Yet there are four hundred thousand Indians in Durban, more than half of the Indians in the entire country.

Symanthia risked those critical stares in order to attend a keep-fit class during her school holidays. "It was held at Claridge's, one of the big beach-front hotels. It's an international hotel, which means non-whites can go in. When I went to the class, they were quite surprised. They didn't expect an Indian. I wasn't so sure before I went that there wouldn't be a problem, but everything was fine. I'm quite at home, everybody's friendly. This was the first time I had ever gone to something for whites before. When I go into that hotel, people do look at me. Well, I look back at them. It happens especially when I get into the lift, because usually I'm the only non-white, and it's full of whites. The area where the hotels are is only for whites. You don't see many Indians besides the waiters and other workers. So when they do see an Indian girl, I suppose it's something different."

In all the beach-front area, there are no hotels for Indians. In all of Durban, with its four hundred thousand Indians, there are no facilities for this race group, except one lower-class hotel, far from the beach front. An Indian who wants to vacation at the beach must travel away from Durban's popular beach front, to a hotel well south of the city; it's a long drive from the restaurants and amusement parks that attract so many whites to the shore. If Symanthia wants to spend the day at the beach, she goes to the Indian beach, the Blue Lagoon, which is next to the beach for whites.

Though Indians are prevalent in Natal, there aren't any in the province next to it, the Orange Free State. By law, they aren't permitted to live there. "Dad was traveling through the Orange Free State and he got stuck there for the night. He had to sleep in the car, because Indians aren't allowed to stay there overnight." Still, the family feels that life is easing for

Indians in South Africa. Today they have their own university, Durban–Westville, which is for Indians (only about a dozen students of other races have permits to study there). But having their own university does present one drawback. "Before we decided to build our house in Reservoir Hills, I

would have preferred to study at the university here in town. But they wouldn't accept me because I am an Indian. It would make a difference if we could associate with other races. You are able to understand different people and their different way of life if you are able to discuss it when the groups are together. It's really at university that you make a lot of friends. It's the only time that you could get to know other races—but I don't have that at Durban–Westville."

Symanthia's chosen field of study is an odd one for an Indian; it's the teaching of Afrikaans. "A lot of my friends disapprove of my studying to teach Afrikaans, but they haven't much say in the matter. This is my choice. I've managed to convince most of them that Afrikaans is an interesting subject and it's what I like doing." In South Africa, Afrikaans can be a kind of passport, opening doors that are closed to the predominantly English-speaking person. Those who speak the language find easier passage through the white, Afrikaner-dominated bureaucracy. Though Afrikaans is required for all students, many forget what they've learned when they leave school.

Because Afrikaans is compulsory, the Indian school system needs many Indians to teach Afrikaans. In South Africa, below university level, whites teach whites, Coloureds teach Coloureds, blacks teach blacks, and Indians teach Indians. So Indians like Symanthia learn Afrikaans in order to teach it to other Indians. Though the government insists that all be bilingual in English and Afrikaans, they are equally determined that the Indians should be kept separate and develop separately among their own people. For those Indians who do not work for or with Afrikaans-speaking whites, learning the language is simply an exercise. "Perhaps two out of ten Indians can speak Afrikaans. For quite a few of the jobs on the beach front, they take Indians, but you have to speak Afrikaans. When I hear an Afrikaner speaking Afrikaans, it isn't exactly the same. With their accent, you don't understand everything they say. Some of the lecturers at the university are Indian, but the white lecturers, if you speak to them in Afrikaans, get quite thrilled about it.

"Very few of the students seem to be interested in Afrikaans. They do it because it's compulsory. As soon as they've completed matric, none of them will even look at Afrikaans. It's not compulsory in university, you choose your own subjects. So, few choose it." Because the government needs Indians to teach Afrikaans to Indians, however, they encourage students to take it as a course of study by offering a bursary (a scholarship). With the bursary she receives, Symanthia will get four years of free education. Otherwise, the family would have to pay R2,000 ($2,300) for her tuition. "We get a special allowance for books as well. When I graduate, I have to work for four years as an Afrikaans teacher. That is a way of paying the government back for the bursary. If I teach less than four years, we have to pay back for each year less. It's quite fair."

What isn't fair is the government's pay scale for teachers. The South African government never forgets that Symanthia is an Indian. As an Indian teaching Afrikaans, her salary will be lower than that of a white teaching Afrikaans, about 25 percent lower. A Coloured teaching Afrikaans earns slightly less than an Indian; an African teaching Afrikaans earns about half what a white earns. Yet they all teach the same subject at the same level.

Symanthia and her family are not totally isolated from whites. Her father, a bookkeeper, works for an English firm that makes no distinction among its employees with regard to race. "There is no racial discrimination in his company whatsoever. You are judged only by your ability to do a job. And the offices, the rest rooms, are all mixed. I've been to Christmas parties at the office for the children of the employees and I've even been to one of the parties for the adults, where we danced with the whites. They asked us to dance and they didn't feel we were different. We often have these friends to our home and they have meals here from time to time." Symanthia's mother, too, enjoys contacts with whites in her job as a private secretary for an English air-conditioning firm.

While some people of color in South Africa are beginning to feel a kinship of oppression with the blacks, many at the same time fear the blacks. "In 1949, when my mother was just nine years old, there were some riots. It was the Africans [blacks] who were fighting for freedom and they went for the Indians first, they attacked all the Indian areas first. It was terrible. It was as though they were in a state of war. Our family couldn't leave their home at night, the place had to be kept dark. My granny saw lots of Indians being killed by the Africans. By comparison, very few whites were hurt." Records show that fifty-three Indians and

eighty-three Zulus were killed. Since the police intervened, who killed whom is open to conjecture.

"If the majority were allowed to vote, I suppose an African would come to power. It's possible here. I think that might be even worse for us, because an African would kick us out, like in Uganda. Somehow the Africans are prejudiced against Indians—they don't like Indians—because we have more opportunities. I think that's the first thing they would do. I would rather live as we are and hope that things will change. What we would really like is equal job opportunities, equal pay for work done, freedom to go to different places, freedom of movement. I'd be happy if we had that, without the vote." It's a safe, limited dream. And it's a dream that could come true for the Indians, for South Africa needs more and more educated people to fill skilled positions. Unwilling to allow more than just a trickle of blacks into these key positions, the country turns to less threatening groups like the Indians. It provides a university in which to train them and offers bursaries for those who choose the right subjects.

Yet, while Symanthia diligently applies herself to her Afrikaans studies, she cannot speak Tamil, the language of her forefathers. Over the 120 years since the Indians first came to South Africa, much of the culture and language of their ancestry has been lost. Many Indians live within the confines set out for them by the government, paying the price for a cultural identity that is no longer theirs. Symanthia's family was in this situation until three years ago. "Here in South Africa we have drifted away from our culture. Many people have given up praying. They don't light the lamp any more, which we must do every day when we pray. We pray through Bhagavan Sri Sathya Sai Baba. He is our guru, our spiritual leader. We learned about him from people who visited India, about the miracles he performs. His movement in India brings people back to praying. He has made us aware of our loss. We began praying again, and now we are making an attempt to learn Tamil. Every evening before the sun sets, we light the lamp, and then we pray at it. Thursday is our holy day. On that day, we don't eat meat at all. I know that many in India and even here in Durban are vegetarians all the time, but I suppose we've taken on more of the Western outlook. We eat meat, but not on Thursday. We never eat pork or beef, only mutton and chicken."

Symanthia experienced her own religious conversion with her whole family when they witnessed, over a period of seven weeks, the growth of a bread brought from India by an aunt. Each week, tea was poured into a tray with the bread, and at the end of each week the bread was divided into two. At the end of seven weeks, there was seven times as much bread as when they started. "We saw this happen. We also saw ashes on these photographs in our home, on the face of Sai Baba. Everybody saw it. That night, we had a prayer at home, and quite a lot of people came in and prayed. After that, we went down to the Blue Lagoon, where we put the bread on a banana leaf and sent it out to sea with a light burning on it. The light burned until we could see the leaf no longer. And from that time, we became followers. On Thursday, when we pray, we give fruit and food at the lamp as an offering. And after we pray, it's blessed food, so we distribute it to others. Actually, Sai Baba's religion isn't really much

different from that of other Indians; he has just brought us back to our religion."

Now Symanthia would like to make a pilgrimage to his *ashram*, a holy place where people gather to study and meditate, as her parents did recently. "It was the first time anybody in our family had ever been to India. And from what they have told us, I definitely want to go there with my two sisters. The *ashram* is near Bangalore, which is the area my great-grandparents came from. Of course, we don't have any relatives in India any more, but my parents have made friends who we would like to visit. It is because of Sai Baba that I would want to go. I don't think my parents would have even gone to India otherwise, that was the only reason for going."

Being of Indian ancestry, Symanthia and her family have no difficulty in getting visas to India, visas which are denied to other South Africans. It's a retaliatory move, perhaps, for the 1913 Immigration Act that prohibited Indians, among other race groups, from immigrating to South Africa. That act made it impossible for foreign-born spouses of South African Indians to enter South Africa. In 1978, this prohibition was repealed.

One of the most distinctively Indian sights in Durban is the big Indian temple. Symanthia frequently attends services there since the family began actively to follow their Hindu religion. "Sometimes we go to a service just here in Long Street, where all the Indian shops are. There's a lady who does the prayer every Thursday, and she gets into a sort of a trance and she blesses you. Then there's a service. So while we have a prayer in our home, once in a while we do go out to a prayer there."

At the same time that the family began to pray to Sai Baba, the girls began to study another aspect of their long-lost culture. Now they would like to travel to India to see and study classical Indian dancing. "We dance in traditional Indian dress. We have the pants that are full and tied around the ankles, and on top we wear the *kurthas* that are tied around the waist. When we're having a class and practicing, we wear leotards. It's very formal, very stylized, like ballet. There's special music that we dance to, much of it was taped in India. There are a number of South African Indians who went to India and graduated in classical dancing and then came back and started classes here. So we became encouraged to take up dancing. My sister Michelle, who is twelve, has become most involved. She recently placed second in a competition and hopes, when we go to India, to stay there to study seriously. Then she, too, would come back to teach here in Durban. And this is all part of coming back to our culture. Now I want to study Tamil, so I can speak our language as well. It was Sai Baba who inspired us to find our religion, our culture, and our language."

Though many Indians have lost contact with much of their culture, the taboo against intermarriage of different castes remains very important. "According to the government, an Indian can marry a Coloured or an African, because we're all considered non-white. But even now, I know young people who can't marry because of caste. I know a Hindustani who has fallen in love with a Tamil and they can't marry. And Muslims very

116　　SOUTH AFRICA

seldom marry out of their religion. If they do, the non-Muslim has to convert, even if it's the boy. I do have Muslim friends and I get on with them, they mix and are very friendly, but when it comes to marriage, that's very different. They go their own way. Before they marry, they'll go out with a Hindu girl, a Tamil girl, like me, but they won't marry her."

In the streets of Durban today, Indian women in Western dress outnumber those who wear the sari, but married women wear the traditional red dot on the forehead, to indicate their marital status. Girls like Symanthia wear saris for special occasions. "I love wearing a sari. We wear it for weddings and on Thursday when we have our prayer, and to go to weddings. Whether it's to go to a white wedding or to an Indian wedding, I wear the sari. It's very dressy, and I feel very elegant and smart and very feminine—I feel Indian, definitely. There is special jewelry to go with it, and makeup as well. We dress completely Indian. It is in a way like putting on our culture when we wear the sari."

The Indians of South Africa aren't in the sugarcane fields any more. Those jobs are held by black Africans now. The Indians are the shopkeepers and the bookkeepers, the tailors and the office workers. Some of them own the sugar plantations. Symanthia will become a teacher of Afrikaans and pass along the Afrikaner's language to other Indian children. Little by little, she'll find a few more amenities open to her as an Indian. If she doesn't ask for much, she will live comfortably in South Africa. But a glare from a white on a bus reminds her that some will always judge her by her skin, by the tilt of her beautiful brown eyes. She remains, uniquely, a South African Indian.

Eight

Debbie Hermanus

Cape Coloured

T<small>HE</small> S<small>OUTH</small> A<small>FRICAN</small> government's obsession with race sometimes leads it into vague areas where labels do not stick easily. Such is the case with the peoples of mixed race. When two races mix, the result is a third kind of person, someone who is a bit of both, yet not all of either. Such mixtures have occurred throughout history, when two peoples intermingle as a result of military adventures or economic explorations. When the Dutch arrived at the Cape in 1652, they mixed with the Khoikhoi, creating the first Coloureds. The mixture was then complicated by the arrival of the Malays and later the blacks. These mixed people originated at the Cape and have no other home. If the policy of separate development was carried out in a logical and consistent manner, these people would have claim to most of the Cape peninsula.

The Coloureds still constitute the work force of the Cape, which was declared a Coloured labor preference area in 1966. Because there were enough Coloureds there to fulfill the whites' labor needs, the government felt justified in closing it to any more blacks seeking work there. So the

faces of the workers at the Cape are Coloured, whether they are repairing roads, picking grapes, or bringing in the fish at the harbor in Hout Bay.

To make the separate-development policy work, the government enacted the Group Areas Act, designating certain sections of towns or districts as

Coloured or Indian or white. As in the case of the Indians, many Coloureds have been moved to make way for whites. About 700,000 of South Africa's 2,400,000 Coloureds live in the Cape peninsula and are designated "Cape Coloureds." They constitute about half of the total population of the

peninsula. Although their housing is now outside the center of Cape Town, their influence on the feel and look of the city was considerable.

The spirit of the Coloureds, as a people, is reflected in such communities as Woodstock and District Six, where, until recently, whites and non-whites lived side by side. These districts, with their street markets and lively clubs and restaurants, had a special vitality. District Six is part of history now; it was proclaimed "white" and demolished under the Group Areas Act. In the more than ten years since its demolition, nothing has been built to take its place. All that remains is block after block of rubble, and here and there some Coloured squatters who have no other place to go. Woodstock has been left in mid-destruction. Some houses were demolished but others, across the street, remain occupied. Whites and Coloureds still live side by side, but their days are numbered. Both Woodstock and District Six are within a five-minute drive from the heart of Cape Town itself.

The Coloureds have their own fairgrounds and amusement park in Athlone, just outside Cape Town, one of the biggest areas designated for Coloureds in the Cape. They go to their own beaches, often right next to the beaches for whites, though the facilities are usually inferior. If they choose to join the army, they become part of the Cape Coloured Corps. In every way possible, the Coloureds are channeled to live apart, and not to share in the same life with whites. This leaves them in a position of unique strain: they know they are a result of the mixing of white and non-white, yet each of those groups rejects them. The whites reject them because they are a reminder that racial mixing was condoned by their ancestors; the blacks reject them because the Coloureds have far more privileges than they, while carrying some black blood. The Coloureds are truly the people in-between. Even their most important cultural event, the joyous Coon Carnival, reflects a bizarre mix of rituals borrowed from the American minstrel tradition.

Debbie Hermanus is a Cape Coloured, born of Coloured parents in Woodstock, a section of Cape Town. Debbie's mother was born of a marriage between a Coloured man and a white woman. They were married before the government passed the Prohibition of Mixed Marriages Act in 1949, which made marriage between whites and other race groups illegal. But when the Group Areas Act of 1950 forced the races to live in separate,

designated areas, such couples could no longer live legally as a family. Coloureds in South Africa say apartheid legislates against love that crosses the color bar. But even families that were all Coloured suddenly found they didn't have a right to live where they had always lived.

"When Woodstock was declared a white area," Debbie relates in her soft-spoken way, "we had to move out. My parents had lived there all their lives—my mother was born in that same house where we lived when I was born. She had lived there for thirty-six years. But now they said it was for Europeans [whites]. After we moved, they knocked our house down, and the other houses on our street, too. But across the street, those houses are still there, and the people are still living in them. And they never built anything where our house used to be. It's just the way it was when they knocked it down. I don't understand why they did it." Such relocations are going on all over South Africa. Sometimes the rebuilding programs are not yet financed, though the removal programs are.

"We didn't have any choice about where we went then. They just moved us into Hanover Park, one of the Coloured areas not far from Cape Town. It was bad there; the kind of people who lived there were really rough. There were always people drinking and fighting, the windows were always being broken. Mother was afraid to let us play outside." Debbie and her family were experiencing one of the biggest social problems among Coloureds—alcoholism.

At that time, Debbie's younger sisters and brother were quite small and still needed their mother's care. But the need to get out of that neighborhood was even greater, and her mother decided to go to work. "My parents wanted to buy their own house so we could live in a better neighborhood." In two years, with both parents working, they were able to save enough to

leave Hanover Park and move into a house in Athlone. "It costs more to live in this house, the payments are R60 a month, but it's much nicer here. We have electricity, a full bathroom with hot water, a nice yard, and the whole neighborhood is safer."

The only thing wrong with the house, from Debbie's point of view, is that it constantly reminds her she is a Coloured, living in a Coloured community. Already she has grown weary of having every phase of her life guided by her color, and she would dispute her mother, who says, "I'd rather be a first-class Coloured than a third-class European." Debbie won't admit it, but in the choices she makes, she's turning her life away, as much as possible, from those activities designated for Coloureds.

For two years, Debbie played with the Western Province Women's Field Hockey Association team. She was the youngest player on the all-Coloured team and held the key position of goalkeeper. For those two years she gave her energies to the club team. Her hockey career culminated in a nation-wide contest held at the old diamond-mining town of Kimberley, where Coloured teams from all over the country competed. Debbie was one of twenty women chosen to represent Western Province—the western half of the sprawling Cape Province. Her reward was the highly coveted springbok emblem, the top award given to sportspeople throughout South Africa, in all sports.

When Debbie took up her stick and ball for a bit of informal practice, suddenly she came alive, spiritedly playing with the ball all alone. Yet, when she returned from Kimberley, Debbie said, "I'm resigning from the team." Debbie claimed that in her final year at school she could not devote that much time to hockey. "I have to do my matric studies now. I can't do both." But in a subsequent conversation she said, "They wanted me to be goalie again. I would rather play on the field, instead of waiting in the net. It's too much of a burden to be a goalie. And they wanted me to be away for a week in June for another special tournament. I couldn't do it." So many reasons—but perhaps none of them the real one—which is that her love of the game was overshadowed by the need to pull out of an all-Coloured team in an all-Coloured competition.

Her teammates, she admitted, would be very disappointed when they found she had resigned from the club. Typically, Debbie submitted her

resignation by letter, very formally. Though adamant about her decision, she confessed, "I'll miss it when the season starts."

Most body-contact sports in South Africa remain rigidly separated by race. This policy is the main reason behind the International Olympic Committee's 1964 decision not to permit South Africa to compete in the Olympic Games. For the players, there is always the question, "Would we be good enough to beat a white team?"

In one sport, marathon running, the participants have been able to answer that question. Sometimes organizers apply for permits to run multi-racial events. Debbie got up at four o'clock in the morning one Saturday, to help out at a multi-racial marathon race. Her schoolwork took a back seat because she chose to get involved in an event where she could be just a person, not a Coloured. The event, the annual Two Oceans Marathon,

traces a course for fifty-six kilometers (about thirty miles) around the Cape peninsula, following a course that touches the Indian and Atlantic Oceans.

Debbie's neighbor Jimmy, the father of her boyfriend, works for one of the sponsors of the stands that dotted the course, providing water for the

runners. Though he was paid for his efforts, Debbie's were strictly voluntary, and she worked hard, filling big plastic containers with water, then tussling with them to load the truck. The multi-racial crowds that lined the route cheered the runners on, and when the leaders came into view near her stand on the breathtaking curves of Chapman's Peak Drive, Debbie could see a white and a black running shoulder to shoulder, leading the more than 750 runners.

It was a happy day for Debbie, and a welcome break from her school studies at Kensington Senior Secondary School. "The school is pretty far from here, about forty minutes by train. Usually I get a lift with my physical-training teacher, so it takes about half an hour. I wouldn't mind if I had to take the train all the time. I'd go there anyway. It's a much better school than the ones here in Athlone; the teachers here just aren't interested. At Kensington, they're a bit strict, but they're very good." The school is for Coloureds, of course. And since the family has to pay school fees, whether Debbie goes to the school in Athlone or in Kensington, they'd rather get

the most for their money. Education is free only for whites. Coloureds also have a higher student-to-teacher ratio than whites: it's thirty to one for Coloureds, and twenty to one for whites. But it's fifty-two to one for blacks. South Africa spends money to support education, based on race: $740 for each white; $217 for each Indian; $160 for each Coloured, and $47 for each black.

Debbie starts her day early, studying from five until six in the morning. "I prefer to study in the morning. Then I leave for school at seven o'clock." Like all South African students, Debbie takes English and Afrikaans. While some Coloureds speak English as their native language, more than 90 percent speak Afrikaans as their first language. This puts them in a curious relationship with the Afrikaners. They are the only other people in the world who speak Afrikaans as their mother tongue. This is just one of the facts that make many Coloureds wonder why they must be kept so separate.

"At Kensington, my English has really improved. And that's going to be a big help to me because I intend to go to work as soon as I finish my matric exam." Debbie had been thinking of going to the university to become a teacher, until she found out that she would be restricted to teaching only Coloureds. Also, she would have to take her degree at the University of the Western Cape, where the language of instruction is Afrikaans. "It's the only university I can attend as a Coloured, unless I want to take a course not offered there, like medicine. Coloured teachers are paid less than white teachers. That's because our standards are lower. We take a different matric exam than the whites do, even though we're in the same province.

"When I go to work, at least people will care about my skills. That's why I'm taking business courses at Kensington. I want to work in a bank when I finish school. I went to Standard Bank in Cape Town with my mother. And they told us that they will give me an interview after they see my mid-year grades." Debbie's chances of getting the kind of job she wants at a bank like Standard are quite good. At Barclays, the biggest English bank in Cape Town, more than fifty Coloureds are employed, many of them in positions in which they deal with the public. Such Cape Town banks draw their customers from a cosmopolitan mix of people, unlike the big Afrikaans banks, which cater to the Afrikaans-speaking community.

Many banks have made it a policy now to pay their staff according to their education and not according to color. Those who come in with a first-class matric pass get a better starting salary than those with an ordinary pass. Debbie has her eye on one of the main downtown banks in a busy commercial area of Cape Town. "I would like to work in a bigger bank because you can learn more there. I'd rather deal with the public instead of sitting in the back just working with papers." The bank will be a kind of island for Debbie, an island where color doesn't matter. But when she wants to have lunch, reality will intrude. In South Africa, restaurants are still largely for whites only. Coloureds can buy food to take out in most restaurants, but they may not sit down in them to consume it. Like most Coloureds, Debbie will eat her lunch on a park bench, or in the employees' lounge at the bank.

In many areas of her life, Debbie remains separated from whites, but the benches at bus stops are no longer marked for whites or non-whites. And in Cape Town, most buses are integrated, a move necessitated by economics. The cost of maintaining separate buses for whites and non-whites became an untenable financial burden. Debbie rides the bus to visit her grandmother, who lives in a Coloured neighborhood near Woodstock. "My grandfather was darker than Granny, and when he died, the authorities told my granny she could move to a white neighborhood; they said she could become white." Her grandmother, who had one white parent, looks white. In South Africa, looking white is one of the criteria for being classified white. "But Granny said, 'No, thanks. If I become white, I'll be separated from my own children. We couldn't go anywhere together. They couldn't come to see me if I got sick and had to go to a white hospital. I've been Coloured all my life, and that's how I'll stay.'"

For Debbie, there is no question of changing her classification. Though she's fairly light in color, her features are definitely mixed. And her search for an identity is not unique. Before the Group Areas Act, the Immorality Act, and the Mixed Marriages Act were passed, the Coloureds looked to the whites for their identity. They spoke the same language, Afrikaans; they shared some common ancestry; they lived a "civilized life"; and some even had the vote. In the Cape, there had been a limited acceptance of the Coloureds as voters, but this ended in the 1950s, when the last loopholes that had permitted them to vote were closed. Many Coloureds, in their frustration, disappointment, and despair over these acts, have turned their backs on the whites. Some think the only answer now is to throw in with the blacks. But Debbie concurs with her mother, who says, "If the blacks take over, then I would rather die than live. We just don't get along." For Debbie, associating with the blacks in an effort to gain rights seems hopeless since the blacks have far fewer rights than they. She wants to compete with whites, who have all the rights. And she's on her way.

When Debbie completes her studies and writes her matric exams, she will have distinguished herself. Only a handful of Coloureds take and pass the matric each year. When Debbie enters the banking world, she'll be making one of the few important decisions in her life where color does not determine the outcome.

Nine

Mthokozeni Khyzwayo

Zulu gold miner

Through the centuries, the allure of gold has spelled mystery, intrigue, and even murder. But for the men who mine it, gold means nothing more than a monthly paycheck. One of the newest parts of the great gold-mining machine is Mthokozeni Khyzwayo, a Zulu from a kraal in KwaZulu, the Zulu homeland. When Mthoko (his nickname) presented himself at the office of TEBA, The Employment Bureau of Africa, which recruits mine labor, he started on a path followed annually by the five hundred thousand men who work the gold mines of South Africa. On that path he would meet men from Lesotho, Swaziland, Botswana, and Mozambique, all countries neighboring South Africa.

TEBA operates recruiting offices in all these countries. With little employment available at home, even countries that have the coolest relations with South Africa still send much of their labor there. New miners and those returning to the mines must be processed through TEBA before they go to work. The men pour into the mines, to work on contracts

averaging nine months. Because of this migratory labor pattern, the turnover each year is more than a hundred percent.

The migratory pattern of labor dates back more than eighty years. Only seven years after gold was discovered on the Witwatersrand, a 350-mile arc of land in the Transvaal which today produces more than half the world's gold, a mine-labor recruiting organization had been set up. Then as now, at the end of each contract period, the men returned to their kraals, to plant crops, to marry, to father children. On an average, they make three trips, rarely spending more than a total of two and a half years in the mines. The average age of the gold miners in South Africa is twenty-five. Sixty percent of them come to the mines with absolutely no formal education. Most miners have been herdboys, looking after the family's cattle; to many rural blacks, cattle mean wealth.

Blacks are migrant workers, while whites build careers at the mines. The white miners' union is the strongest union in South Africa and has successfully kept black miners in inferior, low-paying positions. The black miners face a dilemma of their own as well. Since many tribes hold land communally, once a man leaves with his family, he loses any rights to that land. And blacks may not own land outside the homelands.

Until 1974, three-quarters of the black mine workers in South Africa were foreigners. South African blacks could find other low-paying, non-skilled jobs, without having to resort to working underground. Mine wages, however, increased fivefold in the mid-1970s, when the price of gold rose from $35 an ounce to more than $200 an ounce. As the recession dried up other jobs, South African blacks began to flow to the mines, eventually supplying more than 70 percent of the labor. The gold mines, though not government-controlled, felt it was in the best interests of the country to employ local people in preference to foreigners. But Zulus, the largest ethnic group in South Africa—numbering more than five million—are sparsely represented. Zulus go reluctantly to the mines. One of their strongest taboos is never to be "deeper than the graves of their ancestors."

Before he went to the gold mines, Mthoko tried other jobs in Durban, nearer to his home, but they brought him little money and offered nothing for the future. His lack of skills and practical training made him unfit for anything but manual labor. It was at his father's insistence that he finally decided to become a gold miner.

Mthoko's kraal, the group of structures in which his family lives, lies quite near the east coast of Natal, on the Indian Ocean. As a young boy, Mthoko was almost entirely on his own. His father, who works as a security guard at the gold mine, was away for a year at a time, only coming home on annual leave. He is one of the few black miners who has made mining a career. Mthoko's three brothers, all older than he, have good jobs in Durban, seventy miles south of the family kraal. The oldest works in a bottle store, the next oldest is a bricklayer, and the third works in a large hotel as a chef's assistant.

Traditions of rural life, and Zulu standards, are changing as the need to enter the cash economy becomes more urgent. Mthoko, his little sister, and their mother were the only ones living at home. None of Mthoko's brothers stayed home to look after him, as is traditional in Zulu culture. Being of a carefree nature, he chose what seemed the easiest path. He spent most of his time playing with his friends, visiting them at their kraals. Because there was no adult male at home, the family did not keep cattle, only fowl that his mother could take care of. Mthoko had no responsibilities and simply enjoyed himself, taking long walks to see his friends and spending the whole day with them as they tended cattle.

None of these boys went to school. But when he was twelve, Mthoko decided to go to school. "I wanted to learn to read and write," he explains, so he asked for money from his mother and went to school, about a mile away from the kraal. He learned to read and write Zulu in the three years he was there. "I left then because I really did not like school. I can read and write very well. I can read the Zulu newspaper easily." Had he stayed in school longer, he would also have learned to speak some English. He did manage to pick up a few words, even in that short time.

Since Zulus don't live in villages, they take their addresses from the nearest important building. For Mthoko, this is the trading store in Maphumulo. Home to him is a group of five large, separate structures, all belonging to his family. Each is a circular room, built of stones held together with mud, made very smooth, and then painted. The sloping roof is made of thatch, supported by a network of poles. Meals are prepared in a separate kitchen, used only for cooking. There is no ventilation in these rooms, so the smoke from the cooking fire fills the kitchen. The floor of each room is made of earth and dung, pounded to a finish so hard and smooth it has the feel, underfoot, of cement. The floor is then painted and polished. In Zulu tradition, the boys sleep in their own room. Because his brothers are not at home, Mthoko sleeps alone. "My sister is little, so she stays with my mother and my father, when he is home."

Mthoko's life in the kraal follows a simple routine. "Each day I get up and take a basin of water from the kitchen to wash my face. Then I dress, usually I just put on some rough clothes, overalls. I keep all my clothes in a trunk. When I get up, I take the reed mat I sleep on and roll it up. And I put the blankets away. Sometimes I have to go out to cut some wood for the house, to fix a gate or the roof before breakfast. I always have mealie meal porridge for breakfast." Mealie meal is made from corn, the staple food of blacks. As soon as breakfast was over, Mthoko left for the day. He didn't even bother to come home for a midday meal, preferring to spend time with his friends. "We just talked as we walked about with the cattle." And so it went for Mthoko. No cares, no work, little schooling, little supervision. Life in the kraal suited him.

But as he grew older, Mthoko began to want money. And to earn money, he had to leave KwaZulu, where there is little work for either the skilled or the unskilled. The time had come for Mthoko to cast off the blanket rural people use instead of a coat, and leave the kraal behind. His life would change dramatically once he left that familiar circle. No more would his father trim his hair as he sat outside in the clearing. No more would he live in his own room, his mother close by to prepare his meals. Because a friend of his had become a houseboy in a white home in Durban, he decided to try to find a similar job. Zulus often become houseboys in South Africa. It's a term that can cover everything from cooking to cleaning to gardening, depending on the individual and the household. It is also applied to men of all ages.

Having made his decision to look for work, Mthoko informed his *induna* —the senior tribal representative—of his intentions and left. But a black in South Africa is not allowed just to go to the city to look for work. Reference

books and influx-control laws were established to prevent them from doing so. Mthoko didn't bother to apply for permission to seek work in Durban, however. "If I saw any police van in Durban, I'd just hide in the yard until they went past. I didn't really worry about it."

Armed with one English sentence, "I am looking for the job," he began knocking on doors in Durban North, a well-to-do white suburb. "That was where my friend was working. I'd have a look at the house and the yard first, and if it looked nice, I'd try there. I thought I would like working in a house like that. While I was looking for work, I stayed with my friend." Because he stayed with a friend, Mthoko had no worries about food or lodging. But he was breaking the law. Only registered servants may live on the premises of a white household. They may not bring their wives or children, and certainly not friends.

The search went on for two months. Every day, Mthoko went out to try to find work. "I would go to about fifteen or twenty houses a day. I really wanted to become a houseboy, so I didn't get discouraged that it was taking so long to find a job." Then one morning he knocked on the door of the house of an elderly Afrikaner couple. The woman who answered the door told him to come back that day at noon, when her husband would be home. When he returned, the couple decided to take him on. "They spoke very good Zulu," he explains, "so there wasn't any problem because I couldn't speak English or Afrikaans."

Before Mthoko could start to work, his pass book had to be put in order. The couple took him down to the local office, where the movement of blacks into the area is controlled. He was fortunate to get permission to stay. He could have been arrested, or fined for violation of the pass laws; or he could have been "endorsed out," that is, sent back home to his kraal. Instead, his status was legalized and his employment began.

"We didn't discuss salary at all. My friend was earning forty rand a month [$46] and had been working for four years, so I thought I'd get about twenty-five or thirty rand." But after the first month, when he received his first pay packet, Mthoko got a terrible shock. His salary was only R15 a month. "I didn't say anything. It was my first job, the first place I ever worked in. So I just carried on like that. But I thought it was very low." Now he says the salary was low because the couple was retired, so they couldn't afford very much. And that's probably why they agreed to hire a boy off the streets and take him into their home.

"The old lady was very nice to me and she taught me how to do things, how to polish and wash up. I worked from seven in the morning until six-thirty, with an hour off in the afternoon. And I had half a day off on Wednesday and all day on Sunday." Mthoko quickly adjusted to the requirements of the job, and though everything was very new to him, he encountered no more serious problems than an occasional broken teacup.

The work wasn't very demanding, so for the while at least, he was content. And on Sundays he could satisfy his craving for contact with Zulus.

"At least twice a month, on Sunday, I walked to the Kings Mead Stadium, close by to where I was working. The Zulu dances are held there, and teams from all over come to perform." In Zulu dances, men act out traditional stories, almost always culminating in a dramatic fall to the ground, to simulate a death in battle. Because he knew the stories, Mthoko could follow those dances as if they were plays. "The dancing reminds me of the stories I've heard about the Zulus, how they were very powerful in the past. I know the Zulus were great warriors." So, for a few hours on a Sunday afternoon, Mthoko was a Zulu among Zulus. His life revolved in a simple pattern of work and recreation.

As the months went by, he had to accept the fact that his job wasn't leading anywhere. After a year as a houseboy, Mthoko hadn't advanced a rand in salary. So one day he simply said he was leaving, and he walked out. "I didn't ask for more money and they didn't offer any." Although he had wanted to be a houseboy because he didn't think he'd like to do manual labor, little else was open to him. With no education or experience, Mthoko had nothing to offer but his hands. His brother found him a job at the building firm where he was employed. There Mthoko worked as an unskilled assistant, simply passing tools and materials to the workers as they did their jobs. Again, it was a low-paying, dead-end job.

Meanwhile, Mthoko's father was preparing to return home on his annual leave from the gold mine. He was concerned about Mthoko's aimlessness and wanted to see him, the youngest of his four sons, settled into a good position. And Mthoko, too, wanted to find some work that would pay better and in which his lack of education and training could be overcome. He decided to go to the gold mines with his father. "When my father first went to the mines, I was just a baby. And everybody who lived near our kraal laughed at him." They thought he was going against Zulu tradition. Until recently, there were only four thousand Zulus among the half million gold miners. Mthoko's father did not, in fact, go against Zulu tradition, since his job as a mine security guard keeps him on the surface.

"They laughed, but he didn't mind. My father kept quiet through the years, and now they see where he has gotten because of it." Each year,

Mthoko's father returned from the mines laden with goods, the kind of goods that are out of reach for those who stay in a traditional cashless society. The money his father sent home, month after month, year after year, ensured the family sufficient food, warm clothes, blankets. So Mthoko made the decision to become a miner. When his father came home that year, Mthokozeni—the name means "to be pleased"—agreed to return with him to the mine. His father, who had given his son that name, now had reason to be pleased himself. His youngest son was following in his footsteps.

His father had come home at this time in part because Mthoko's little sister had been badly burned with boiling water. To ask the ancestral spirits for help, his father slaughtered an ox and a goat as part of a ceremony of appeasement. This ceremonial slaughter and the gathering of the family at the kraal marked one of the few formal occasions in Mthoko's life. Though the Zulus enjoy a very strong tribal pride, they do not have the rich lore of initiation and other rites that some tribes do.

When his father's month-long leave was over, the two set off for the mines. As a returning employee, his father had only to report to any TEBA recruiting office and say that he wanted to resume work. In addition to recruiting, the offices are the link between the mines, the miners, and the families of the miners. They are located in the areas the miners come from,

so wives can easily walk in to ask for help in contacting their husbands, or to look for mail from them.

When Mthoko showed up at the TEBA office in Tugela Ferry, in the heart of KwaZulu, he was started on a well-organized process that would bring him to a gold mine just two days later. The local recruiting officer put Mthoko through the paperwork. Fluent in Zulu, he gave Mthoko a rundown on what life was like at the mines, what he would earn, the opportunities there, and what would be expected of him. Mthoko's employment forms were filled out and his pass book checked. He spent one night at the TEBA hostel and in the morning appeared before the local magistrate to attest to his willingness to work in the mines. After his fingerprints were taken, Mthoko dropped into the local trading store for some last-minute purchases. These are South Africa's general stores, selling everything from food to clothes, pots and pans, and blankets.

Though Mthoko could have been assigned to any one of the forty-five gold mines that rely on the recruiting organization for labor, luck was on his side. He was assigned to the same mine his father works at: Blyvooruitzicht (*blay-for-'ate-zik*). This mine, whose name means "Happy Outlook," is only an hour's drive from Johannesburg, in the gold-mining arc of the Witwatersrand. Mthoko's journey to the mine began with a long bus trip from Tugela Ferry. Supplied with tickets that would take him all the way to Carltonville, where the mine is located, Mthoko boarded the bus with his father. "It's a long ride because the bus picks people up all along the road. The hills are very steep and the road curves a lot, so the bus goes very slow. It took us four hours to get to the train station where we had to wait for the train to Johannesburg." At each change of transport, a representative from TEBA was at the station, making sure that none of the men went astray. Because so many can neither read nor speak English or Afrikaans, and may be traveling on their own for the first time, they need help to reach their destination. "At Johannesburg, we had a long wait for the train to Carltonville. We ate at the hostel in Johannesburg while we were waiting. Finally, we got to Carltonville."

Carltonville is the site of one of the deepest mines in the world and is one of the most intensely mined areas in the Witwatersrand. The entire countryside is filled with mining operations. Each mine shaft is topped with a headgear, the vital gears and pulleys that drag the ore up from underground and that operate the big elevators the men take to the working levels. The gold-mining process creates tremendous amounts of waste material, which piles up in dumps. The dumps form mounds that look like artificial mountains across the horizon. Mine hostels stretch out in long, low lines around the mines. This is Mthoko's new world, a world filled with men and machinery.

Twelve thousand men work at Blyvooruitzicht; all but twelve hundred of them are black. Men from twenty-six ethnic groups work together there, living in hostels, twenty to a room. By law, only 3 percent of black miners may be housed at the mines with their families. Though this saves the mines the cost of providing homes, they are burdened with the massive costs of retraining, a process that goes on every time a man returns to the mine, and with the cost of transporting him home and back. Many of

the mines would prefer to house their black workers and be able to maintain a stable work force.

Mthoko was stunned by his first days at the mine. "I had to learn everything. They showed me how to get around, where to go to eat, where to get my pay, where the shops are." At each change of shift, thousands of men come tumbling out of the mine, heading for the vast kitchens, which are open at this mine twenty-four hours a day, so that food is always available. The miners do not eat while they are underground, where the heat and humidity drain a man's energies. When they come up, they want a good meal, and then some native beer, a thick brew with the taste of sour milk.

Mthoko's mates are all Zulus. The custom at the mines is to house each

ethnic group in a separate room, though there may be several groups in the same hostel. Some hostels house several thousand men.

Because the men are largely illiterate, special tests have been devised to determine their general abilities and what jobs they are best suited for. Mthoko scored quite well on his tests, high enough to be able to advance quickly if he shows ambition and interest. Salaries are paid according to responsibility. A man who operates an expensive piece of machinery is paid many times more than a simple laborer.

As soon as the testing was completed, Mthoko was taught Fanagalo ('fan-a-ga-lo), the common language of the mines. With so many groups coming together, each speaking its own language, a basic common language was created to enable the men to communicate. When miners work underground, communication can mean life or death. Fanagalo is a Zulu word meaning "like this." The language covers basic, practical matters. "It took me six days to learn Fanagalo," Mthoko says, conversing easily with the interpreter. He had the advantage over other miners, since Fanagalo is based on Zulu, the most widely used language in southern Africa, and the base of an even larger language group. "I enjoyed learning it because now I can speak to anybody at the mine, no matter what tribe they are from. I can talk to the men in the kitchen and to the other men in the hostel." Equally important, he can understand the instruction he is given.

Once he had mastered Fanagalo, Mthoko began his practical training, learning the names of the many tools used at the mines, tools he had never seen before. Mthoko works well with his hands, a very useful attribute at the mines. Mining is a complicated business. Some men are at the actual drilling site, called the stope, where the rock face is prepared for blasting. Others work hauling up the ore that is blasted loose. Still others work aboveground, in the recovery plant, where the ore is crushed and processed to release the gold. Eighty-five percent of the men work underground in some capacity. The rest provide the services needed to keep the hostels running and the machinery in repair.

At the training ground, miners become familiar with the tasks they will be performing when they go underground. Here, on the surface, they learn the routines; they have to learn them well because in most of the

work areas the only lights are those on the hard hats the miners wear. Instead of a sunny sky overhead and a pleasant breeze, there is a kind of perpetual night, and the men sometimes work in spaces only a few feet high. They crawl along the drilling sites, where wedges of wood help absorb the tremendous pressure bearing down on the rock.

To demonstrate to visitors some of the jobs open to miners, Mthoko was allowed to try out several jobs at the training site. He operated the winch that scoops up the ore once it has been blasted loose; he crawled up a simulated mine shaft, where new miners become familiar with underground conditions. Then he was taken in hand by an instructor, from Botswana, who explained the workings of the *loco*, a little train that transports ore to the elevator shaft where it is taken to the surface. "I really like this job," Mthoko exclaimed, as he was shown the motor of the *loco* and learned how it was operated. For a first-timer like Mthoko, this job is still out of reach, however. He needs experience in the mine and maturity before such a job would be entrusted to him.

During this first phase of his employment, Mthoko has been assigned a surface job, working with a team of men. Their job is to replace the liners in the giant drums that tumble the gold-bearing ore and break it down to workable size. This takes a full day and is done once a week. For the rest of the work week, Mthoko and his teammates do general cleanup

work in the reduction plant. Because he is on the surface, Mthoko earns R11.70 a week ($13.25). If he goes underground, even as a first-contract worker, he will earn R17.70. Many men, even Zulus, choose to go underground on their second contract. As soon as he has passed the training period, his wages will go up. The workers are given their lodging and meals, and transportation at the beginning and end of their contracts. To keep them occupied during the long stretches between shifts, films are shown several times a week. Traditional dancing, like the Zulu dances Mthoko enjoyed in Durban, are one of the most popular forms of entertainment for the miners.

Going to the mines is a new ritual for Zulus like Mthoko. In ways both large and small, it is a change from family life back at the kraal. Traditionally, Zulu men do not marry before they are thirty-three. It usually takes that long for them to earn *lobola*, the bride price which is almost universally required by Africans and which can be as much as R1,000 ($1,150). A miner who saves his money can accumulate that much in one or two contracts, so Mthoko could marry by the time he is twenty-two or twenty-three, and return to the kraal.

"Being away from home doesn't worry me. When I worked in Durban, I didn't see my family for more than six months. And my father is here. I see him about once a week. And my cousin is in my hostel, in the same

room. He is my best friend here, so I'm not lonely. I'm saving my regular pay, they keep it for me here, and when I go home, I'll have it all to take with me. I work about two hours overtime a day, so I use that money for myself. That's how I bought this watch."

Like so many thousands of worker bees, each miner does his own job, not knowing how it all fits together. He doesn't know that the ore being blasted loose today will travel up to the big recovery plant. The worker in the plant sees the rocks moving past him on a conveyer belt and doesn't know that there is gold trapped in them, gold that will be released through a series of crushing operations that will lead to a cyanide mixture in a huge vat. And only very few, black or white, actually see the molten gold pouring red-hot from the furnace down a trough and into a bar-form.

Mthoko knows nothing of these processes, though they are happening all around him. Like the typical miner, who describes his job as "pulling money from the ground," and who thinks it's white men's foolishness to be digging like this, Mthoko really doesn't connect his work at the mine with gold itself. He looks at a gold ring worn by a visitor and shakes his head. "I don't know what it's made of."

Ten

Basil Johnson

Boy on the border

When Basil Johnson set off for the train station one morning to begin his military service, he didn't have a very clear idea of what it would be like for him when he did his stint "on the border." But he did know he would be going to the border, even before he began his two-year National Service duty. "Everybody goes to the border," says Lance Corporal Basil Johnson, who prefers to be called B.J.

The "border" separates Angola from the territory called South-West Africa/Namibia. The two names give a clue to the transition the land is undergoing. More than fifty years ago, following the First World War, the League of Nations granted South Africa a mandate over South-West Africa. Since the League was disbanded, the question of South Africa's continued right to rule the territory has been in continual dispute. Those most concerned with its status, the South-Westers, or Namibians, have had the least to say about it. In recent years, a group called the South-West Africa People's Organization (SWAPO) has taken matters into its own hands, initiating a guerrilla action in the northernmost part of SWA/Namibia,

Ovamboland. (The name derives from the Ovambo people, one of the major ethnic groups in the territory.) Some incidents have occurred in the interior, including an attempt to blow up a railroad bridge, and the assassination of black leader Clemens Kapuuo, who was killed in the black township of Katatura, just outside Windhoek, the capital, but most of the action has been limited to the section of border that stretches some two hundred miles across SWA/Namibia, closest to the densest black population.

Like most National Servicemen, B.J. was trained to do border duty. "I was sent to Middelburg, for my training. That's just a few hours' drive from Johannesburg, where I live. We get a lot of training, and we learn everything. There aren't so many guys in our army, so we can't afford to have someone who's just a cook or something like that. We all have to know how to shoot, how to defend ourselves." After nine months of training, B.J. and his unit were sent to the main camp at Oshakati, about twenty miles from the border. His unit was among the first group of South African National Servicemen to serve for two years. The war has escalated as a result of the independence of Angola in 1975. With the black-majority regime in Angola cooperating, SWAPO has been able to maintain its bases in southern Angola, striking at SWA/Namibia just across the border.

On the way to the border, B.J. didn't have a very clear idea of what the action would really be like. All the way up, he and his mates exchanged bits of information gleaned from discussions with other soldiers who had already been there. "One guy says you hit land mines every day, you get shot at, there's mortar attacks every morning. And another guy is ten kilometers [about five miles] up the road and there's nothing there. But everybody forgets about what he says, so before we came up here, we sort of think—the border, it's a very unsafe place." Soon enough, B.J. had his own story to tell, and the word "contact," used by the soldiers to describe an actual exchange of gunfire with the "enemy," suddenly had meaning for him.

From the base camp, just three miles south of the Angola border, B.J. and his mates were out on patrol. A patrol could last a few days or a week. Weapons at the ready, they walk through the *bundu*—the bush. The vegetation is dense up here in Ovamboland, where water is not as scarce as it is to the south. And the bush makes good cover for guerrillas. Each evening, as dark descends, the patrol digs in for the night, sleeping in the open, in an arranged pattern. The attack came before dawn. "It was about five o'clock in the morning; ten past five, to be exact. We were all sleeping, and the next thing you know, there's a shot. It's instinct, you just duck, you lie flat. You don't wake up and jump up and have a look around, you just freeze. You wake up like that . . . you're asleep, and the next thing, you wake up and you're wide awake. The first thing you do is you think, 'This is it.' Your heart just stops, it freezes. And the guard screams, 'Okay, get them, go mad, let's go.' I was lying on my back, and the next thing, I was lying on my stomach and I was firing away. You sleep with your rifle, it's your wife. It was a surprise really, because we usually sit and watch the north, toward Angola, because that's where the most likely attack would come from, that's where we've been always told to look. And they came from the damn south, they came up from behind us, so they were pretty close before we realized that there was anything there."

The attack took place in a half-mile-wide strip of land that forms a no-man's-land, two hundred miles long, between SWA/Namibia and Angola. To separate the civilian population from the guerrillas, the South African army cleared out the Ovambo who were living on that strip of land.

Then they put up a barbed-wire fence to mark the actual border. Before, the Ovambo would move easily across the border, which to the tribe is an artificial barrier. They have always lived on both sides of the border, and consider themselves neither Angolan nor Namibian, which are political separations; they are all Ovambo people.

B.J. doesn't know how many guerrillas, or "terrorists" as he calls them, were firing at his patrol. "You don't worry about that. All you know is that it's a lot of gunfire. And then you just start shooting." With tracers from the enemy bullets coming over them, he and his mates began to shoot in the direction of the gunfire. Physically, the men were at their lowest point as the pre-dawn exchange began. "It's a good time to hit a person, you don't expect anything like that. Your reaction . . . of course you've done a lot of training, your reaction is very fast. But you have to have somebody to break the freeze. You lie like that until you hear somebody scream, 'Okay, shoot, shoot, shoot.' And then you turn over and you start, you just go in the direction of the heavy fire. They're hitting above our heads, about a foot and a half. It seems to come down like rain. You can see the tracers. You can see the bullets coming down like that, and you know your time isn't too long, you know you must get those guys before they get you. Because they can see where the bullets are going and they're going to get the range. A terr [terrorist] doesn't know how to judge distance, he always shoots above your head, thank God.

"The next thing you know, you're still in shock, you're still shooting, the whole time you're just going bang, bang, bang, bang bang, the whole time. Then you stop, you think, 'Jesus, I've gone through three magazines, and we've only got six or seven on us.' That's not very many bullets. Then you freeze again. You think, 'I've got half my ammunition gone,' and you start shaking again. Then you use a calm head and you remember all your training."

After a few minutes that seemed like hours to B.J., the battle subsided. "They shoot and they run back and they shoot and they run back and they shoot. You can't really hear it, because your ears are ringing the whole time. It took about six minutes, the whole thing. And then you lie there. You don't watch the time, you just lie absolutely still. You don't get up, you just wait for it to get light." Slowly, the night receded, and a faint glow of light

came up. B.J. strained to see if SWAPO soldiers were around. The faint
light grew into daylight. "You're lying there the whole time, stiff-armed,
ready, watching. The time doesn't matter. And you just start thinking,
'This is it. This is what I came for.' You think, 'Okay, I've been in a
contact. I know what it feels like. It feels exciting . . . great.'" Now it
was really daylight. "You're all jittery then. You start smoking. I don't even
smoke, but I smoked that day. A guy says, 'Ha, ha, ha,' he doesn't laugh,
he just says it. Some kids are pretty bad. You've been in it now, and it's
not very nice. You think, 'This is what I came for, this is really what I came
for.' You're happy and you think, 'Thank God. Here I am, tomorrow is
another day for me.' You're really happy for yourself for coming through.

"You never know if you've hit anybody, the way everyone is firing.
We wouldn't know because they never leave a body, they always take them
with them. But we could see the tracks where they had dragged two guys

away. And with the bullets we use, when they hit . . . well, you can just figure it out for yourself."

For most National Servicemen like B.J., the contact was an exception. Much of the time, the boys are waiting and watching, looking for an enemy who is invisible, who maintains no camps on the SWA/Namibia side of the border. Even though the war has escalated, most soldiers do not have any contact with hostile forces. Most soldiers do not fire their guns except in practice.

B.J.'s understanding of the border war he is fighting is minimal. "If you ask any little chap in South Africa, any schoolboy, he knows about SWAPO, he knows that there's an organization called SWAPO. And they are an irritating bunch of chaps. That's what they tell you at school." For B.J., the Ovambo who comes at him with a gun from across the border differs in only one respect from the general Ovambo population. "A uniform and a rifle, that's the distinction. If they've got a uniform and a rifle, you shoot them. If they haven't, you can't do a thing about them. Look, it's difficult. You meet a civilian [Ovambo]. You can help him, you can give him biscuits. Then he can run back, tell his mates all about us, and off we go. We've got our contact for the night. You're very unsure."

The SWAPO soldiers who are fighting to gain control of their country cross over the border at night to stage their strikes. They slip back again before light. They are, largely, an unseen enemy who attack the unarmed civilian population in a campaign of intimidation far more often than they fight South African soldiers.

During their patrols, the South African soldiers talk to the local people, using an interpreter. They ask about any SWAPO soldiers they might have seen. "After a while you can feel there's trouble in a kraal, that the people aren't right. You can feel the attitude toward you. I don't know, I can't really explain it. You just have to live in this place to really understand." Those patrols mark B.J.'s first real contact with blacks. Up until now, he has seen blacks only as servants at home. Now he sees them as the enemy, undistinguishable, except for the uniform, from the people he is told to protect.

It was during an interview with a SWAPO prisoner, conducted by one of the officers, that B.J. came face to face with an articulate, educated black. The prisoner, identified only as Willy, was captured during a raid by the

South African army on two SWAPO bases in Angola. In addition to destroying many weapons, the South Africans killed an undisclosed number of men and took two hundred prisoners. Willy was one of them. B.J., who listened intently during the questioning, appeared to be both uneasy and fascinated by this man, who quietly described the April 1978 raid in which he lost his right arm. B.J. seemed unable to connect Willy with his own concept of the black as laborer, servant, uneducated enemy. He heard Willy discuss the political aspects of the fight to free SWA/Namibia; heard him disassociate the political party of SWAPO from the fighting arm. Afterwards, all B.J. could say was, "He's been well coached."

SWAPO is not the only group fighting for control of Namibia. Other political parties continued to hold rallies in SWA/Namibia as both the war and the debates continued. South Africa and the United Nations have been trying to work out plans leading to free elections, while the war goes on. But South Africa appears unwilling to permit completely free elections; they fear SWAPO would win, and a SWAPO-controlled regime in SWA/Namibia is unacceptable to South Africa.

For soldiers like B.J., the political maneuvering is unimportant. Their concern is only with danger, and boredom. Yet the war has brought B.J. the greatest responsibility of his life. "When you're coming into the *veld*— the fields—you must remember everything you've been taught. The last time we came up, I was a recce—reconnaissance man. I was in front with binoculars, rifle, grenade, all of that. You're always looking around and you've got a lot of responsibility when there's ten, twelve, maybe twenty guys behind you, just out of sight. If you walk past thirty terrorists lying there, and you don't see them, they're going to leave you alone and they're going to sock it to the guys coming along later. And then you've just killed some of your friends."

There is danger for the soldiers not only in the bush but on the roads leading to it, for the guerrillas lay mines in the roads to blow up vehicles. Because of this, mine-proof transports carry the soldiers from the camp at Oshakati to the semi-permanent camps close to the border. Nicknamed "Biffles," these vehicles, with their V-shaped bodies, deflect the impact of a mine. The soldiers, held in securely by intricate seat and shoulder belts, come through unharmed. The vehicles do have one drawback—they tend

to roll when the hard dirt roads become soft during the rainy season. B.J. knows firsthand what that feels like.

"We took a corner at about thirty kilometers an hour. We could feel it start to tilt and it tilts and it carries on tilting. You look at your friend next to you and you say, 'Hey, Tommy,' and you grab him and you duck. Thank God we were all strapped in. You just see the ground coming over you and it stops, there's smoke, and everybody hits their belts to release them and they fall out and some guys get stuck. Then we're all joking and I hear one guy, he says, 'Hey, Basil, old chap, would you mind giving me a little kick out of here.' I looked under there, he's sitting there upside down with his strap on. So I ran in and hit his belt and whoosh he goes to the ground and very formally he says, 'Thank you,' and he crawls out."

When the soldiers are not out on patrol, they spend time guarding the field camp, watching from the guard tower for any sign of the enemy. The semi-permanent camp is surrounded by bunkers, with sleeping tents and mess tents inside. Meals are a welcome break in the day, but even more welcome are letters from home. "If I don't get a letter, I just don't feel like doing anything. If you get letters, you're happy on the border. My girlfriend Gail, she writes me almost every day, but the way the mail comes up here, I might not get anything for a week. Then on a Monday there's seven letters." There really isn't much else to do. The camp is just a place to rest between patrols, to pick up new supplies, to get ready to go out again. By the end of the five-month tour, the men are eager to go, to have their leave. With the increased action, however, more soldiers will find themselves going back to the border for a second five-month stint, as B.J. did. "It's a lot, really, ten months up here."

B.J.'s grown up a lot since he first took that train from Johannesburg, leaving behind his folks, his two sisters, his car, and his dog. Does he miss

them? "I miss everything at home. You miss everything, because you lived like that for eighteen, nineteen years before you went into the army, and that's the way you like to live. All of a sudden, you're getting up at four in the morning." Still, going back won't be a problem, he thinks. "The first day you're home on leave, you fall right back in. People say it's hard, but it isn't. But your social life goes for a loop. That is the most difficult to get used to. That chap who was in your class in matric, who went to university when you went to the army, you find he's not on your level any more. I'm not saying that university guys are immature, but they haven't been through things you've been through. You look at things from a different view. You don't look at it like a schoolboy. You sit and you think about something and then you give an answer. You think about life more seriously. Most people say the army makes a man out of you, that it either makes or breaks you, and it's true."

Going to the border is a part of the life of every white South African boy today. As B.J. sees it, he's defending his own country. "If we lose up here on this border, we're going to be fighting on our own border next." The rights of the Namibians to determine their own future, to be in control of their own lives, never enter into the picture. For B.J., it's a simple matter of fighting to preserve the South African status quo; he's fighting to uphold apartheid.

Epilogue

WHEN OUR YEAR of work in southern Africa was completed, we found people there turning to us for advice. "How soon do you think things will change here?" they asked us. We think things will stay as they are for years to come. From our reading of the history of South Africa, from our conversations with South Africans of all colors, from our year of living in the situation, we could only conclude that, with the strength and determination of the government and the weakness of the separated people, the situation is most likely to remain as it is.

Though the world outside clamors for change, though it seems to Americans that South Africa is a volatile powder keg that threatens to explode at any moment, it does not look that way from inside the laager. Afrikaners still debate about allowing even the smallest, least significant change. When a rugby stadium in Pretoria was opened to all races in October 1979 for a world heavyweight boxing championship, in which black American John Tate beat white South African Gerrie Coetzee, the event received worldwide attention. But for black workers like Mthoko, even the least expensive ticket cost half a week's wages. Blacks still face formidable opposition in their struggle for significant change.

For those who read the newspaper, change would seem to be the daily bread of South Africa. In the brief time since we first met the young people you now know so well, South Africa has changed her Prime Minister, her President, her Minister of Justice, and other important officials. Yet the basic policy of apartheid remains the same. The faces of authority have changed but the fact of authority has not.

The real changes are in the lives of the people, and in the lives of "our kids." Kathy successfully completed her matric exams and was accepted for an American Field Scholarship in South America. Dewe wrote his matric exams and passed on the highest level, and was thus guaranteed a place at any white South African university. He chose instead to fulfill his National Service requirements first, and is now serving a two-year term in the South African Navy at Saldanha Bay in the Cape. Symanthia completed her first year in university with good grades and a very full schedule. Her parents decided to go ahead and build a new home in the Indian section outside Durban, and hope to be living in it shortly.

B.J. spent his final three months of service at Messina, on the border with Zimbabwe Rhodesia, before returning home. He is now enrolled in university, where he hopes to earn a degree to teach physical education at the high school level. Crossroads was not torn down, thanks in part to

intensive campaigning by the English-language press. Princess became pregnant and is now raising her baby in her parents' home in Crossroads.

Lukhetho left his job at IBM to further his education at the university level. Mthoko completed his training period at the gold mine and is nearing the end of his first contract period. Debbie successfully completed her high school studies and is pursuing a career in a Cape Town bank.

We look forward to hearing from them all from time to time. Even as South Africa continues to apply its energies, its resources, its manpower to promote and further the idea of apartheid, its people continue to live their lives. These lives, these stories are what happened in South Africa, the laager, yesterday.

Ettagale Lauré
Jason Lauré
New York City, October 1979

Glossary

Afrikaans—language of Afrikaners, derived primarily from Dutch; one of two official languages, with English

Afrikaner—white descended from early Dutch, French, and German settlers

apartheid—policy legislated by whites to enforce total separation of the races and ethnic groups

banning—legislated policy to prohibit social contact and sharing of ideas; usually for a period of five years; can be renewed indefinitely

bantu—people; formerly used by whites to refer to blacks

bantustan—*see* homelands

Boer—farmer; formerly used to denote Afrikaners

Coloureds—people of mixed race who are indigenous to the Cape Province

detention—government policy of holding a person in prison without lodging a charge for an indefinite period

homelands—land reserves, designated by the white government, for blacks; based loosely on black ancestral territories; formerly called bantustans

kaffir—derogatory term for blacks, similar to the American word "nigger"; derived from Arabic word for unbeliever

Khoikhoi—cattle-raising people who lived in South Africa before the first whites arrived kraal—traditional black-family compound

laager—defensive enclosure used by Afrikaners; now a metaphor for a defensive frame of mind

lobola—traditional bride price paid by black men

matric—comprehensive exam required of all high school students to obtain graduation certificate

mealies—ears of corn; staple diet of blacks

native—word formerly used by whites as derogatory reference to blacks; predates use of "bantu"

pass—work record blacks are required to carry at all times; also called "reference book"

rand—unit of currency, equivalent to US $1.15

San—nomadic people who lived in South Africa before the arrival of the whites

Sotho—black ethnic group constituting country of Lesotho; QwaQwa and Lebowa are Sotho homelands in South Africa

swartgevaar—black peril; denotes whites' fear of being overwhelmed by black majority

Swazi—black ethnic group comprising country of Swaziland; Kangwane is Swazi homeland in South Africa

Tswana—black ethnic group comprising country of Botswana: Bophuthatswana is Tswana homeland in South Africa

veld—rolling farmland or countryside

Voortrekkers—group of Boers who journeyed into interior of South Africa in seventeenth and eighteenth centuries

Xhosa—black ethnic group whose ancestral land constitutes homelands of Transkei and Ciskei

Zulu—largest black ethnic group in South Africa, numbering more than five million; ancestral home is KwaZulu

Acknowledgments

During our year in southern Africa we were helped by many, many people, such as the man who drove out of his way to help us find Mthoko's gold mine, and the Inkatha members who introduced us to Lukhetho. Some we came to know quite well; others remain nameless. To all of them we offer our sincere thanks for helping us accomplish our work.

We appreciate the thoughtful comments and criticisms of Susan Hall of the African-American Institute, and hope the finished work reflects the improvements she suggested.

Grateful thanks go to our interpreters, who translated not just words but also cultures for us. Special thanks to Bill Larkan in Tugela Ferry for the many hours we spent with him, and for the hospitality extended to us. We appreciate also the efforts of TEBA's Bill Exley at the Blyvooruitzicht mine.

In Crossroads, we pay special tribute to the courageous and cheerful Muriel Mbobosi. For his insights and practical help during our work at the "border," we thank Major Andy Anderson.

Finally, we thank "our kids," for letting us share their lives. This book is really for them: Lukhetho, Dewe, Debbie, Symanthia, Kathy, Princess, Mthoko, and B.J.